When Friends Gather

Sharing the Joy, Comfort, and Food of Friendship

Susan West Cannon

Special Delivery Publications
Lubbock, Texas

ISBN 1-885620-05-5
First Printing   November 2002 5,000

Cover designed by Dell Cannon
Antique print from private collection

Published by
Special Delivery Publications
5109 82nd Street, Suite 7, #204
Lubbock, Texas 79424-3099
1-800-533-8983
www.whereheartsgather.com

WIMMER
COOKBOOKS
ConsolidatedGraphics
1-800-548-2537

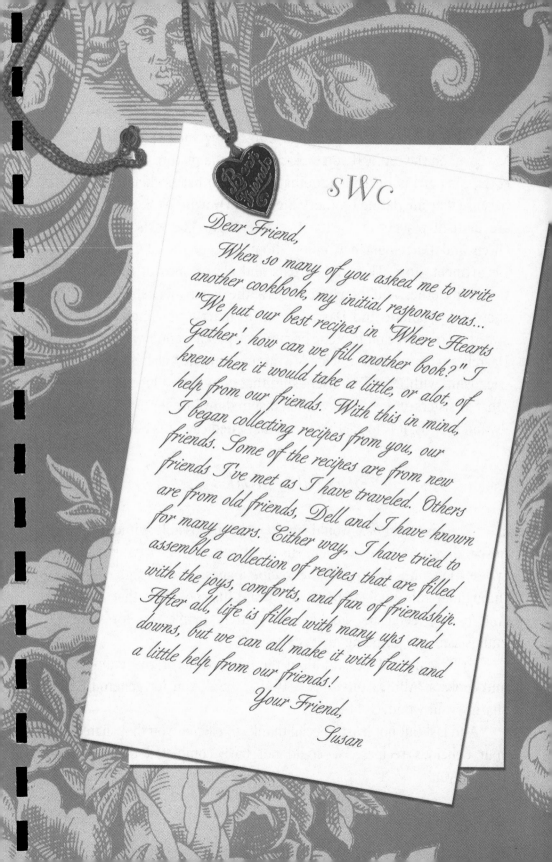

sWc

Dear Friend,

When so many of you asked me to write another cookbook, my initial response was... "We put our best recipes in 'Where Hearts Gather,' how can we fill another book?" I knew then it would take a little, or alot, of help from our friends. With this in mind, I began collecting recipes from you, our friends. Some of the recipes are from new friends I've met as I have traveled. Others are from old friends, Dell and I have known for many years. Either way, I have tried to assemble a collection of recipes that are filled with the joys, comforts, and fun of friendship. After all, life is filled with many ups and downs, but we can all make it with faith and a little help from our friends!

Your Friend,

Susan

The story behind the picture...

The year is 1950, young girls in bobby socks listen to "All My Love" on the radio. If you look closely at the picture on the back cover, each girl is wearing a football charm on her necklace. That's because they are dating brothers; Steve and Dwayne West. Both boys are football players at Carter-Riverside High. The girls, Jeanette Owen and Darrell Barney, enjoy shopping together at Stripling's Department Store. They try on hats and gloves, look at the latest trends in clothes, and then have lunch at the department store coffee shop. Both Jeanette and Darrell go on to marry their high school sweethearts. Steve and Jeanette became my parents and Dwayne and Darrell my aunt and uncle. My mom Jeanette, cherished her friendship with Darrell. A friendship that grew into a love for each other as sisters-in-law. Both women inspired my love for home, family, and friends. It is to each of them, that I dedicate this book.

Special Thanks

This cookbook would not have been possible without my husband and best friend, Dell. His creativity on the cover, patient typesetting and layout of the recipe pages, and design work throughout this book make it the beautiful cookbook that it is! And to my teenagers, Logan and Kaitlyn, thank you for your enthusiasm and for being my taste testers!

To Rosemary West, and all of the talented decorative painters and cooks at All Seasons Arts & Crafts, thank you for generously sharing your wonderful recipes!

And last but not least, special thanks to each of you that shared your delicious recipes. We could not have completed this book without you!

Contents

When Friends Gather for Joy

Appetizers 7
Beverages 21
Breakfast & Brunch 35

When Friends Gather for Comfort

Soups 49
Bread 57
Comfort Food 67

When Friends Gather for Fun

Salads 81
Main Dishes 101
Side Dishes and Vegetables 121

When Friends Gather for Dessert

Cakes 139
Pies 153
Cookies 169
Desserts 189

Index 201

*Don't walk in
front of me,
I may not follow.
Don't walk behind me,
I may not lead.
Walk beside me,
and just be my friend.*

Albert Camus

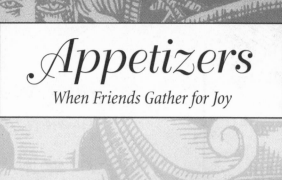

Appetizers

When Friends Gather for Joy

*When just
being together
is more
important than
what you do,
you are
with a friend.*

*S*andy Lindeman of Plainview, Texas, sent us this wonderful dip. It is flavorful and is great for a crowd because it makes a lot! I met Sandy when I was speaking in Plainview to a group of ladies from First Baptist. These ladies all have a heart for hospitality. They are also fortunate to live in a town where people still know their neighbors!

Hospitality is ... friendship in action.

Southwestern Cheese Dip

2½	(8-ounce) packages cream cheese softened
½	cup mayonnaise
¾	cup sour cream
½	cup grated Parmesan cheese
1-2	fresh jalapeños, finely diced
2	green onion, chopped fine
½	red pepper, chopped
2-3	(7-ounce) cans diced green chilies
2	teaspoons ground cumin
2	teaspoons chili powder
pinch of salt	
1	cup Cheddar cheese
avocado for garnish	

In a large bowl, combine cream cheese, mayonnaise, and sour cream until well blended. Add remaining ingredients except Cheddar cheese and mix well. Fold in grated Cheddar cheese. Place in a large glass baking dish. Bake at 350° for approximately 10 minutes or until bubbly and a little brown. Garnish with diced avocados and serve with lots of tortilla chips.

Note: If you are serving a large group you might want to divide this into two baking dishes so you can place it in two different locations. This way everyone will be able to enjoy this crowd pleaser!

Black-Eyed Pea Dip

3	(16-ounce) cans jalapeño black-eyed peas (drained)
1	(3½-ounce) can diced black olives
1	purple onion, chopped
2	cups grated Cheddar cheese
1	(16-ounce) bottle Catalina dressing
3	avocados, chopped
3	tomatoes, chopped

Mix first 5 ingredients together. Refrigerate overnight. A couple of hours before serving add the tomatoes and avocado. Stir them in to the dip. Serve with corn chips.

Note: I like to add the avocado right before serving. This way it is really fresh and the color is still good. Choose the rough bumpy skin avocados, they have the best flavor!

When shopping for avocados, choose ones that yield slightly when pressed. They should also be heavy for their size and not be blemished. Do not purchase the ones that are too mushy.

Store ripe avocados in a cool spot for up to 2 days or in the refrigerator for up to one week.

This dip is incredible! The recipe is from Mary Krablin of Spring, Texas. I had the pleasure of meeting Mary and attending her "Christmas Creations" Home Show with my friend Juli McArthur. What a treat! Not only is Mary a gracious hostess, but she is an avid antique collector. Her home was a feast for the eyes! Around every corner was a wonderful surprise.

*T*his is one of Dell's specialties. He uses Haas avocados, the type that have the bumpy skin, and combines them with simple ingredients for an outstanding guacamole! Have your ingredients diced and ready to assemble but do not cut the avocado until right before serving. When exposed to air, the avocado will begin to turn brown. Some people say that placing the seed into the bowl of guacamole helps keep it from turning brown. This may work for awhile, but the guacamole will begin to turn dark. Guacamole is best when served fresh!

Guacamole

2	large ripe avocados
1	teaspoon California-style garlic powder
½	teaspoon salt
2	tablespoons minced onion
1	teaspoon seeded and minced jalapeño
2	tablespoons diced seeded tomato
	juice of ½ lime

Cut avocado in half, remove seed, and scoop out into a bowl. Mash with a fork. Stir in garlic powder and salt. Add remaining ingredients and stir until well combined. Serve immediately.

Serving Suggestion: This is great as a dip with white corn tortilla chips.

Note: This is a repeat from our first cookbook, but it is the best guacamole recipe! It is so good with Dell's Chicken Fajitas on page 110 that we had to include it again.

Stacey's Salsa

1   (14.5-ounce) can diced tomatoes with jalapeños
2   (14.5-ounce) cans diced tomatoes
1   medium onion, chopped
1   (4-ounce) can chopped green chilies
3-5   tablespoons lemon pepper seasoning
3   teaspoons Accent
2-3   teaspoons salt
Fresh cilantro to taste (Enough sprigs to <u>loosely</u> fill one cup)

Put ingredients in food processor and blend until chunky or continue pulsing until it is to the consistency of your liking. (Note: Be careful with the cilantro. It can over power the salsa. It's flavor also increases once it has been refrigerated.) This is one of those recipes you have to adjust to your taste. The first time you make it, you may want to start with the smallest amount of the seasonings and then taste and adjust accordingly.

Note: I like to drain two of the cans of tomatoes before adding to the food processor so the salsa is a little thicker.

My sister, Karen, served this last time we were in Oklahoma and I told her I had to have the recipe! It is from her friend Stacey Knight. Stacey and Karen have been friends since Karen and her family moved to Oklahoma. Stacey and her husband David have definitely been the kind of friends you can count on! They have shared both abundant joys and deep sorrows with Karen & Philip; along with an unwavering friendship!

Stacey has a heart for hospitality and we are so thankful she shared this delicious salsa recipe with us!

Appetizers

*A new favorite!
This is unique and has
a great flavor! A
wonderful dip to serve
as an appetizer when
serving Mexican food or
any entree with a
Southwest flavor!*

*Note: I bake mine in a
rectangular baking dish
or you can use a 9 x 9.*

*A mild delicious
spicy flavor! You can
serve the pecans as an
appetizer or try them on
a salad. Crank up the
spice, if you like, with a
little more cayenne!*

Hot Southwest Corn Dip

2	(11-ounce) cans Mexicorn, drained
1	(7-ounce) can chopped green chilies, drained
1	(4-ounce) jar pimentos, drained
2	cups shredded Cheddar/ Monterey Jack cheese
1	cup mayonnaise

Mix all ingredients together and pour into a pyrex baking dish. Bake at 350° for 30 to 40 minutes. Serve warm with tortilla chips.

Texas Spiced Pecans

½	cup butter or margarine
1½	teaspoons chili powder
¼	teaspoon cayenne pepper
½	teaspoon garlic powder
1	teaspoon Worcestershire
1	teaspoon seasoned salt
3	cups pecans

In a medium saucepan, melt butter and seasonings; add nuts and stir until coated. Spread evenly on a baking sheet with sides. Bake at 300° for 20 to 25 minutes, stirring often.

Turkey Club Rollups

½	cup mayonnaise
4	ounces cream cheese, softened
½	cup chopped, drained pepperoncini (see side note)
2	tablespoons chopped fresh cilantro
4	slices bacon, crisply cooked and crumbled
6	(7 or 8-inch) flour tortillas
½	cup chopped tomato
½	pound thinly sliced turkey
6	leaves of leaf lettuce

In a small bowl, combine mayonnaise and cream cheese; mix until smooth. Stir in pepperoncini, cilantro, and crumbled bacon. Warm tortillas to make them soft and pliable. (Note: You can do this in the microwave by wrapping the six tortillas loosely in wax paper and microwave on high for 30 to 45 seconds). Spread about 2 tablespoons of the mayonnaise mixture on each tortilla. Top each with a rounded tablespoon of chopped tomato, 1 slice of turkey, and 1 lettuce leaf. Roll up each tortilla lightly. Cut each roll into 8 pieces; secure each piece with a cocktail toothpick. Serve immediately or cover tightly and refrigerate until serving time.

Yield: 48 appetizers

Wendy Wallace, my Mom's neighbor, served these at a neighborhood gathering. Mom told me how good they were, and Wendy graciously shared the recipe. I think they would also be wonderful cut in half and served as a sandwich at a picnic or tailgate party!

Note: Pepperoncini are thin, two to three-inch chilies. The ones used in this recipe are pickled and available in a jar at your local grocers.

*T*his dip includes
the classic combination
of bacon and tomatoes.
Serve it with your
favorite crackers or
chips. Especially good
when you use fresh
garden tomatoes.

*A*nother dip that is
especially good when
made with fresh
summer produce. Try it
with the little pickling
cucumbers; they have a
great mild flavor and
fewer seeds.

Note: I like to stir in the
avocado just before
serving so it is fresh
and not turning dark.

Bacon Tomato Dip

10	slices of bacon, cooked crisp, (drain well, cool & crumble)
3	large ripe tomatoes, seeded and finely chopped
½	cup mayonnaise
½	cup sour cream
1	tablespoon Dijon mustard
¼	cup minced green onions
6	drops Tabasco sauce

Fresh parsley, minced (for garnish)

Combine all ingredients in food processor. Process until chopped, but not pureed.

Cucumber-Avocado Dip

1	tomato, seeded and diced
2	cucumbers peeled, seeded, and diced
2	cups sour cream
1	package dry Italian salad dressing mix
1	avocado, peeled and diced

Drain diced tomato and cucumber on a paper towel. Combine the remaining ingredients and chill before serving. Serve with chips or fresh veggies.

Stuffed Cherry Tomatoes

1	pound bacon, cooked until crisp and then crumbled
¼	cup finely chopped green onion
½	cup mayonnaise
2	tablespoons chopped parsley
2	tablespoons grated Parmesan cheese
24	cherry tomatoes

In a medium bowl, combine all ingredients except tomatoes. Stir until well blended. Wash and remove stems from tomatoes. Place on a paper towel for a few minutes to dry. Slice a <u>thin</u> layer off the bottom of each tomato so they will sit up straight. Using a knife or the tip of a vegetable peeler, scoop out a little of the tomato from the stem end. Fill with bacon mixture and chill for several hours.

Yield: 24 appetizers

Serve these on an attractive tray or add them to an appetizer tray for a touch of color!

Appetizers

This appetizer combines the wonderful flavors of bacon and tomato. The cherry tomatoes provide lots of color to your serving table. Val Franks, my sister's mother-in-law, shared this delicious and unique appetizer recipe.

It is mutual respect which makes friendship lasting.

Looking for something different? It's easy to make and is a nice change from the regular chip and dip appetizer. This recipe is from Chaplin Tom Hollingsworth, who was a friend of my Dad's. Daddy liked Tom because he was down-to-earth and was a very thoughtful person. They worked together at Greenwood in Ft. Worth.

Friendship doubles our joys and divides our grief.

Marinated Appetizer

1	(5¾-ounce) can jumbo pitted black olives
1	(7-ounce) jar large stuffed green olives
1	(7-ounce) jar largest mushrooms
2	(14-ounce) jars artichoke hearts, halved

Drain all of these well!

Marinade:

¾	cup sugar
⅔	salad vinegar
⅓	cup salad oil (not olive)
1	teaspoon salt
1	teaspoon coarse ground black pepper

Place drained olives, mushrooms, and artichoke hearts in a large bowl that has an air-tight lid. Combine marinade ingredients in a saucepan. Bring to a boil, stirring until sugar dissolves. Cool slightly before pouring over vegetables. Marinate overnight. Remove ingredients with a slotted spoon and place in a serving dish.

Baked Cheese Dip in Sourdough Bread

1	(10-inch) round Sourdough bread
1	(14-ounce) can artichokes, chopped
1	cup grated Cheddar cheese
1	garlic clove, minced
1	cup mayonnaise
1	cup grated Monterey Jack cheese
1	small onion, chopped very fine
1	cup freshly grated Parmesan cheese
dash	salt
dash	Worcestershire sauce
fresh ground pepper to taste	

Cut a thin slice off the top of the loaf of bread. Set aside. Using a gentle sawing motion, hollow out the bread loaf. Leave ½ inch around the edge and on the bottom of the loaf, being careful not to cut through the bottom. Cut removed bread into cubes. Dip in melted butter and sprinkle with seasoned salt if desired. Place cubes on cookie sheet and bake in oven at 350° for 10 to 15 minutes until lightly browned. While bread cubes are baking, mix remaining ingredients, stirring well. Fill hollowed out bread with dip. Replace top, and wrap in foil. Bake on a cookie sheet at 350° for 1 hour. Serve warm with bread cubes, crackers or potato chips.

This unique dip is not only good, but it is a great conversation piece. The bread bowl serving piece is fun and the dip is delicious! Serve it when the weather turns cool and crisp and friends are all gathered to watch the weekend football game!

Serving Suggestion: Don't toast the bread cubes. Place cubed bread on bamboo skewers and serve dip like a fondue!

*T*hese have an incredible flavor! They are sweet with a touch of spice. Serve them as as appetizer or in a salad. Either way they are delicious.

A great snack mix! Mix up a batch for family and friends. This recipe came via my friends Karl and Liz Langford. It is from Karl's Aunt Bobbie Hatch.

Note: Use small brown paper sacks for individual servings.

Sweet & Spicy Pecans

⅓	stick butter or margarine
⅓	cup sugar
¾	teaspoon cinnamon
½	teaspoon cayenne pepper
½	teaspoon seasoned salt
4½	cups pecans

Melt butter in a large saucepan over medium heat; stir in sugar and seasonings. Add pecans; stir to coat. Spread pecans on a baking sheet. Bake at 325° for 15 minutes; stirring every 5 minutes. Cool completely on waxed paper. Store in an air-tight container.

Texas Trail Mix

4	cups bite-size pretzels
1	(12-ounce) box Chex cereal, any flavor
1	(1-pound) can mixed nuts
1	package dry Ranch dressing mix
½	teaspoon chili powder
½	teaspoon cayenne pepper
½	cup vegetable oil

Mix cereal in a large brown paper bag. Add dressing mix and seasonings and shake well. Add vegetable oil and shake well again. Bake in brown paper bag at 200° for 1 hour. Cool and serve or store in an air-tight container.

Marlena's Spicy Do-Dads

3	cups Cheerios
4	cups Rice Chex cereal
4	cups Corn Chex cereal
4	cups MultiBran Chex cereal
1	large can mixed nuts
1	stick margarine, melted
1	teaspoon seasoned salt
1	teaspoon chili powder
1	teaspoon Worcestershire
1	teaspoon Tabasco

Combine cereals together in a large pan (Marlena uses a large roasting pan). Mix remaining ingredients together and pour over cereal. Stir to coat. Bake at 225° for 1 hour; stirring every 15 minutes.

Yield: A bunch!

I met Marlena Dupre at the Dallas Market. She was there with her best friend, Patsy Kincaid, promoting "Celebrate San Antonio", a best-selling cookbook! All three of us love cookbooks and good recipes! Marlena shared this family favorite. It is great to make when you have a houseful of guests.

Parmesan Glazed Walnuts

1½	cups walnuts
1	tablespoon melted butter
½	teaspoon seasoned salt
¼	cup grated Parmesan cheese

Heat oven to 350°. Spread walnuts in shallow baking dish. Bake 10 minutes. Mix butter and salt, toss lightly with nuts, sprinkle cheese on top, stir and bake 3 to 4 minutes or until cheese is melted.

*My mom met Mabel Hinojsa at Keller Elementary. Her daughter was in Mom's 2nd grade class. Mabel was very active in the P.T.A. and was a wonderful cook!
Note: Use the kind of Parmesan in the can.*

*A*nother great
recipe from the talented
cooks at All Seasons.
This wonderful recipe
comes from Donnie
Josefy of Idabel,
Oklahoma. He and his
wife, Kae, always
brought wonderful
snacks when Kae came
for a decorative painting
class. This recipe was a
class favorite!

These are wonderful to
make, especially during
the holidays. Make a
batch and share with
friends.

Orange Glazed Pecans

2	cups light brown sugar
½	cup milk
2	tablespoons vinegar
4	cups pecan halves
2	oranges (rind only)

Combine brown sugar, milk, and vinegar in a saucepan. Cook over medium heat to soft ball stage (234° to 240° or when it forms a soft ball when syrup is dropped in cold water). Add pecans and stir until pecans are coated. Add grated rind and stir. Spread on waxed paper to dry. Store in an air-tight container.

Note: To use the orange rind only, you need to use a zester or small microplane grater. Use only the thin, colored layer of the rind. The white part is bitter. The zester is pulled across the orange rind removing the zest in thin strips where as the microplane grates the zest into tiny pieces.

*How rare
and wonderful
is that flash of
a moment
when we realize
we have discovered
a friend.*

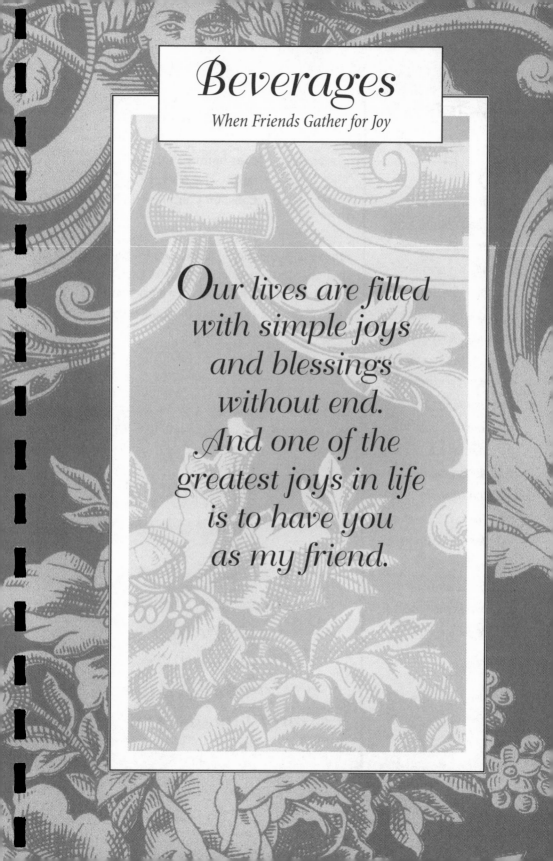

Beverages

When Friends Gather for Joy

Our lives are filled with simple joys and blessings without end. And one of the greatest joys in life is to have you as my friend.

Beverages

*P*am McPherson
and I have been good
friends since college.
Actually we are
distantly related and
consider ourselves
"cousins". In college we
were both Kappas, so
we became sisters too!
Pam served this
delicious tea one
summer as our families
vacationed together. It
was the best tea I had
ever tasted. Pam is a
wonderful cook and like
my mother-in-law,
Naydiene, she can
improve something as
simple as ice tea!

Pam's Tea

4	cups boiling water
3-4	family-size tea bags
1	Constant Comment tea bag
4	cups water

Bring 4 cups of water to a boil. Add tea bags and steep for 5 to 10 minutes. Remove tea bags, pressing out excess water. Pour into tea pitcher and add water according to desired strength. Serve over ice with sweetner and lemon.

Serves: 8

Helpful Hint: To make good ice tea always begin with fresh cold water. Also if your tap water has a bad taste use bottled water.

Let freshly brewed tea cool to room temperature before refrigerating. This will keep it from becoming cloudy.

*Those who bring
sunshine to the
lives of others
cannot keep it
from themselves.*

Fruit Tea

¼	cup unsweetened instant tea
¾	cup sugar
⅛	cup lemonade mix
1	cup white grape juice
2	quarts water (8 cups)

In a 2¼ to 3 quart pitcher, combine all ingredients and stir well. Serve over crushed ice and enjoy!

Serves: 6 to 8

Serving Suggestion: Make fun ice cubes by freezing mint leaves or small lemon wedges inside the ice cubes.

Summer Sun Tea

1	large glass jar
4-5	tea bags
	fresh cold water
	warm summer sunshine

To make sun tea, fill a large glass jar or Sun Tea jar with fresh cold water. Place 4 to 5 tea bags inside. Close lid tightly and place in bright sunlight for at least 4 hours or all day. Pour over ice and enjoy!

Beverages

This refreshing recipe was sent to us by our dear friend, Sue White. It is often served by her daughter Kamber Smith. The tea is easy to prepare and a delightful beverage to serve guests.

If you have never had Sun Tea, try it. The flavor is wonderful!

Beverages

*A*lmond and vanilla combine with ice tea in this wonderful beverage. For years I have enjoyed a hot almond tea (also from my friend Pam), but this cool variation is great when served by the pool or as a cool refreshing punch at a summer reception.

Friends are like flowers in the garden of life- You can never have too many.

Lemon Almond Tea

2	(7-ounce) family-size tea bags
4	cups boiling water
2	lemons, thinly sliced
1	cup sugar
1	tablespoon almond extract
2	teaspoons vanilla extract
1	(2-liter) bottle lemon-lime beverage, chilled

In a saucepan, brew tea bags in hot water for 15 minutes. While waiting for the tea to brew, twist and squeeze the lemon slices as you put them into a large pitcher. Pour in sugar. Add brewed tea to pitcher with lemons and sugar. Stir until sugar is dissolved. (Note: At this point, you can refrigerate overnight or add remaining ingredients and serve right away). When ready to serve, stir in extracts and lemon-lime soda. Serve over crushed ice.

Yield: 12 servings

Note: This also make a refreshing summer punch and will serve 24 to 30 when using punch cups.

Apple Orchard Punch

1	(32-ounce) bottle apple juice, chilled
1	(12-ounce) can frozen cranberry juice concentrate, thawed
1	cup orange juice
1½	cups ginger ale, chilled
1	apple

In a large punch bowl, combine apple juice, cranberry juice, and orange juice. Slowly pour in chilled ginger-ale.

Serving Suggestion: Thinly slice apple vertically, forming whole apple slices. Float slices on top of punch. Remember to dip the apple slices in lemon juice to keep them from turning brown.

Note: Do not substitute lemon-lime beverage in this one. The punch tastes the best with the ginger-ale. My daughter Kaitlyn and I tested this one both ways and the ginger ale definitely had the best flavor.

*L*ooking for something different to serve your guests? This delightful punch is a nice change from the ordinary! A combination of juices create a great flavor and a beverage that is also good for you. This one is so delicious! Serve it over ice to your guests, or use as a punch the next time you are celebrating a happy event!

Beverages

My kids love this punch! It's easy to make and is a pretty red color. Make it festive by using little party umbrellas or use a bamboo skewer to secure the pineapple chunks and cherries.

To choose a good fresh pineapple look for these things.... one that gives slightly when pressed and has a nice golden color. Leaves should be crisp and green. The stem at the bottom should smell sweet. Avoid pineapples with soft dark areas.

One medium pineapple peeled and cored will make about 3 cups of pineapple chunks.

Cherry Cranberry Cooler

2	cups cranberry juice, chilled
1	(6-ounce) can pineapple juice
1	cup orange juice
1	(6-ounce) jar Maraschino cherries
2	tablespoons lemon juice
⅛	cup sugar
1	(12-ounce) can lemon-lime beverage

In a large pitcher, combine cranberry, pineapple, and orange juices. Add juice from Maraschino cherries (save cherries for garnish) and lemon juice. Add sugar starting with ⅛ cup. Pour in lemon-lime beverage and stir. Add additional sugar as desired adjusting to your preference. Stir to mix well. Serve over crushed ice and garnish with pineapple chunks and reserved Maraschino cherries.

Yield: 8 servings

Note: For fun freeze maraschino cherries in ice cubes. Be sure and rinse the cherries before placing them in the ice cube tray so their color will not bleed. Make these ahead of time and store in zip-top freezer bags.

Paradise Punch

2	cups apple juice
1	(12-ounce) can frozen fruit punch, thawed
1	(6-ounce) can frozen lemonade concentrate, thawed
1	(6-ounce) can frozen pink lemonade concentrate, thawed
2	cups water

In a large pitcher combine all ingredients. Stir until well blended. Serve over crushed ice. Garnish with lemon or lime slices.

Yield: 12 servings

Helpful Hint: Place cans of juice in the refrigerator the night before you plan to serve this punch so they can thaw overnight. Also chill the apple juice or make the punch several hours before you plan to serve it so it will be nice and cold.

Beverages

This is my daughter Kaitlyn's favorite! It is a beautiful color and looks very tropical. Just add a little umbrella, sit out in the sun, and close your eyes. You just might feel like you're on a beach in paradise!

The little party umbrellas are available at your local party store. They come in bright tropical colors and add a festive touch.

My mom, Jeanette West, has used this punch for years. It was often served by my Grandmother West, and has been used at wedding receptions for generations. Mom likes this recipe because it is so versatile. She uses it for bridal showers and baby showers. It's pretty yellow color makes it appropriate for both occasions!

Wedding Punch

2	(6-ounce) cans frozen orange juice, thawed
2	(6-ounce) cans lemonade
6	cups water
1	(46-ounce) can pineapple juice
1	cup sugar
2	tablespoons almond extract
2	(12-ounce) bottles of ginger ale, chilled

Mix all ingredients except the ginger ale in a large (4 to 5 quart) container. Place in freezer for several hours. Note: You can pour the punch into smaller containers to freeze it. This also makes it easier to transport and you can mix half of the punch up at a time. You want the mixture to be slushy. When ready to serve put the mixture in punch bowl with an ice ring and add the chilled ginger ale.

Yield: 20 cups of punch

Serving Suggestion: Mom says you can use lemon-lime beverage instead of the ginger ale, but she likes it best with ginger ale.

Making an Ice Ring

1   **ring mold or container that will fit in your punch bowl**
fruit & leaves
water

Place selected washed fruit (strawberries, orange slices, lemon wedges, cherries etc.) in bottom of ring or decorative mold. Be sure to arrange them so the prettiest side is down. Note: If using leaves use a non-poisonous leaf like lemon leaves or simply use washed fresh mint leaves. Add just enough water to cover fruit (this will keep fruit from floating), freeze until firm. It will take about 4 to 5 hours. Fill remainder of ring with water and freeze.

Note: You can even use edible flowers like pansies, roses, or violets in your ice ring. Just be sure they are well rinsed and that pesticides have not been used on them.

Helpful Hint: To loosen ice, dip ring or mold in hot water. Invert and float the ring in the punch bowl.

*I*ce rings are not hard to make, they just take a little advanced planning. My mom makes hers a few days before the party. She also likes to use fruit juice or punch in hers.

*B*e creative! You can also make ice rings in muffin pans or mini bundt pans.

Beverages

How much punch will I need? This is a common question when planning for a shower or reception. Take the number of expected guests and figure 2 cups of punch per guest. A punch cup holds 4 ounces of punch so 1 gallon of punch yields 32 4-ounce servings.

Also remember to consider the weather. If it is a hot summer day you will need to double the amount of punch!

Pretty Party Punch

2	(12-ounce) cans frozen orange juice, diluted as directed on can
1	(46-ounce) can pineapple juice, chilled
2	packages of cherry kool-aid
1	lemon (juice only)
1	(28-ounce) bottle of ginger ale, chilled
1	tablespoon almond flavoring
2	tablespoons vanilla

Mix juices together. Add ginger ale and flavorings. Stir until well blended. Just before you are ready to serve fill punch bowl with crushed ice. Pour punch mixture over ice.

Yields: 1 gallon or 32 punch-size servings

Helpful Hint: Mix together the day before and divide into smaller containers (this will make it easier to carry and transport if necessary). Refrigerate over night so punch is thoroughly chilled. This will keep it from diluting when poured over the ice.

Spiced Apple Punch

4	cups (1 quart) apple juice
4	cups water
1	cup presweetened drink mix (any red flavor)
¼	teaspoon cinnamon
⅛	teaspoon nutmeg
⅛	teaspoon ground cloves

apple slices and cinnamon sticks
for garnish

In a large saucepan, combine juice and next 5 ingredients. Mix well and bring just to a boil. Keep it simmering and garnish with apple slices. Serve in mugs with cinnamon sticks as a stirrer.

Yield: 16 servings

A delicious apple punch that is sure to warm your guests on a cold winter day. Add a fire in the fireplace and some warm hospitality. Your friends will forget how cold it is outside!

Hot Apple Punch

4	cups (1 quart) water
3	Constant Comment tea bags
¼	cup sugar
2	cups apple juice or apple cider

In a large pan, bring water to a boil. Add tea bags and lower the heat. Steep for 5 minutes. Remove the tea bags and add sugar. Stir until sugar is dissolved. Pour in apple juice and stir until well blended. Simmer and serve warm.

Yield: 10 to 12 servings

Another hot punch. This one includes one of my favorite ingredients... Constant Comment tea. This tea has a wonderful spice flavor.

Beverages

*H*osting a coffee or simply having friends over for dessert and coffee? Knowing how to make a good cup of coffee will enhance your hospitality.

Coffees are an ideal way to serve a lot of people. They usually begin in the morning around 9 or 10 o'clock. Muffins or coffee cakes are served with the coffee. For fun, host a "Get-to Know-You" coffee by having each guest bring a favorite coffee mug. Have each one share why it's their favorite!

The Perfect Cup of Coffee

1	clean coffee pot
	fresh cold water
2	level teaspoons of fresh ground coffee per 6-ounce cup

Fill a clean coffee pot with fresh cold water. Note: If your tap water has a bad taste use bottled water. Always use fresh ground coffee. For strong coffee use 2 level teaspoons of coffee per 6-ounce cup. If this is too strong for you adjust to fit your taste.

Note: A standard coffee cup is 6-ounces, but many coffee mugs hold as much as 12 ounces.

Helpful Hints:
Purchase coffee (whole bean or freshly ground) instead of the pre-ground canned variety at the grocery store. The flavor is so much better. There are also several good decaffeinated varieties.

Keep ground coffee fresh by storing it in an air-tight container in your freezer.

Serve coffee as soon as possible or place it in an insulated carafe. You want the coffee to maintain that "first-cup" freshness.

Never reheat coffee; it will taste bitter.

Caramel Chocolate Mocha

4   cups hot brewed coffee
3   tablespoons caramel topping
3   tablespoons chocolate syrup
½   cup milk
whipped cream for garnish
additional caramel and chocolate
syrup for garnish

Stir together first four ingredients in a saucepan. Cook over medium heat, stirring often, until thoroughly heated. Pour into mugs. Top with a dollop of whipped cream. Drizzle with caramel and chocolate.

Yield: 4 servings

Cafe Mexican

½   cup whipping cream
⅛   teaspoon ground cinnamon
⅛   teaspoon nutmeg
1   tablespoon powdered sugar
6   cups of strong black coffee

Just before serving whip first four ingredients together until stiff. Top six cups of strong, hot black coffee with a dollop of this mixture.

Yield: 6 servings

Beverages

A delicious coffee drink that reminds me of the ones served at one of our local coffee houses. This way you can enjoy it at home and also impress your guests!

A quick and easy favorite! This is one you can whip up even when you have spur of the moment guests over for coffee.

See previous page for tips on making good coffee.

Beverages

This makes a great gift for teachers or co-workers. Tie a chocolate dipped spoon onto the jar. Or place the mix in zip-top bags and put it inside a pretty mug. Don't forget to include a tag with the instructions for a single serving.

Another favorite from my mother-in-law, Naydiene's recipe box. Easy to make, this one is great hot or cold! For a cool treat: Chill mixture and serve over a scoop of ice cream. Top with whipped cream and sprinkle with toasted pecans.

Spiced Mocha Mix

1	cup sugar
¾	cup instant nonfat dry milk
¾	cup powdered nondairy coffee creamer
½	cup cocoa
⅓	cup instant coffee granules
½	teaspoon allspice
½	teaspoon ground cinnamon

Combine all ingredients in a large bowl. Stir until well combined. Divide into decorative air-tight containers to give to friends!

Instructions for one serving: Spoon 2½ tablespoons of mix into mug. Add 1 cup of hot water or milk, stir until dissolved. Top with whipped topping and sprinkle with cinnamon.

Viennese Spiced Coffee

10	tablespoons coffee
5	cinnamon sticks
12	allspice berries
¼	cup sugar
½	carton whipping cream
	nutmeg for garnish

Place coffee, cinnamon, allspice, and sugar in basket of a 10 cup coffeemaker. Fill with 10 cups of cold water and perk. To serve top with whipped cream and sprinkle with nutmeg.

Breakfast & Brunch

When Friends Gather for Joy

*A friend is a gift
whose worth
cannot be measured
except
by the heart.*

Breakfast

This is a wonderful combination of flavors and a nice change from the usual egg and sausage casserole. The green chilies are mild so this casserole pleases guests of all ages.

Helpful Hint: Next time you have prepared a large ham and have some left over, dice the leftovers and freeze in zip-top freezer bags. This way you will have it ready when you want to prepare this casserole!

Ham and Green Chile Breakfast Casserole

1	(6-ounce) box herb seasoned croutons
2	cups diced ham
1	(4-ounce) can green chilies
6	eggs
2½	cups milk
1	(10 ¾-ounce) can cream of mushroom soup
salt and pepper to taste	
2	cups grated cheese

Preheat oven to 300°. Spray an 8x8-inch baking dish with nonstick cooking spray. Pour croutons in baking dish. Sprinkle ham on top and spoon on green chilies. In a medium bowl, beat eggs, milk, and mushroom soup together. Season with salt and pepper. Pour over mixture in baking dish. Sprinkle cheese on top. Take a knife and marble cheese into egg mixture. Bake until set, approximately 1½ hours. Serve hot.

Yield: 6-8 servings.

Note: For variation, add:

½	cup diced green pepper
¼	cup sliced green onion
⅓	cup sliced mushrooms

Sausage Parmesan Breakfast Bake

1	pound bulk sausage
½	cup chopped onions
½	cup grated fresh Parmesan cheese, divided
½	cup grated Swiss cheese
1	egg, beaten
¼	teaspoon Tabasco
1½	teaspoons salt
2	tablespoons chopped parsley
2	cups Bisquick
¾	cup milk
¼	cup mayonnaise
1	egg yolk
1	tablespoon water

Preheat oven to 400°. Spray a 9x9-inch pan with nonstick cooking spray. Brown sausage and onions; drain well. Add ¼ cup Parmesan cheese and next 5 ingredients. Stir well. Combine bisquick, milk, and mayonnaise to form a batter, stir in remaining ¼ cup Parmesan cheese. Spread ½ of batter in prepared pan. Pour in sausage mixture. Spread remaining batter on top. Mix egg yolk and water. Brush on top. Bake for 20 to 25 minutes or until it begins to pull away from the edges of the pan. Cool 5 minutes then cut into squares.

Note: You can double this recipe for a 9x13-inch pan or make two because it freezes well.

A delicious breakfast dish. You can prepare the sausage ahead of time and then prepare the casserole the next morning. This is especially good warm out of the oven, but the leftovers are also good when reheated the next day. This dish is a nice change or addition to the sweet breads usually served at breakfast.

Breakfast

*W*ake up to a warm fragrant breakfast cake. This one is easy and delicious! It is yummy for breakfast and also makes a nice light dessert.

Note: Do not substitute a butter flavored cake mix for the yellow cake mix. The yellow cake mix makes a lighter fluffier cake. If you do use a cake mix that has pudding, simply delete the additional package of instant pudding.

Poppy Seed Cake

1	stick butter, softened
5	eggs
½	cup sour cream
1	box yellow cake mix
1	(3-ounce) package instant vanilla pudding
1	cup water
½	teaspoon cinnamon
1	teaspoon vanilla extract
1	teaspoon almond extract
2	tablespoons poppy seeds

Cream butter, with eggs and sour cream. Gradually add cake mix and pudding mix alternating with water. Add cinnamon, vanilla, and almond extracts. Beat for 3 minutes at medium speed until light and fluffy. Stir in poppy seeds. Pour into a greased and floured bundt pan. Bake 45-50 minutes at 350˚. Cool for 25 minutes then remove from pan. Pour or brush on glaze.

Glaze:

4	tablespoons butter, softened
2	cups powdered sugar
2-3	tablespoons milk

Combine all ingredients and beat until smooth.

Note: For a thinner glaze, add milk until desired consistency.

Raspberry Cream Cheese Coffee Cake

2¼	cups all-purpose flour
1	cup sugar, divided
¾	cup margarine or butter
½	teaspoon baking powder
½	teaspoon soda
¼	teaspoon salt
¾	cup sour cream
2	eggs
1	teaspoon almond extract
1	(8-ounce) package cream cheese, softened
½	cup raspberry preserves
½	cup sliced almonds

Preheat oven to 350°. Grease and flour bottom and sides of a 9 or 10-inch springform pan. Combine flour and ¾ cup sugar. Cut in butter with a pastry blender or fork until mixture is crumbly. Reserve 1 cup of mixture. To remaining crumbs, add baking powder, soda, salt, sour cream, 1 egg, and extract. Blend well. Spread batter over bottom of pan and up the sides 2 inches. In a small bowl, combine cream cheese, ¼ cup sugar and remaining egg until well blended. Pour over batter. Carefully spoon preserves over filling. Combine reserved crumb mixture and almonds. Sprinkle on top. Bake at 350° for 45 to 50 minutes or until cream cheese filling is set and crust is a nice golden brown. Cool 15 minutes. Remove sides of pan. Serve warm or cool. Cut into wedges. Refrigerate leftovers.

My cousin, Rosemary West, gave me this wonderful recipe. She said the recipe came from Carol. I assumed she meant her daughter Carol Wheeler, but I thought, "How does the mother of six young children have time to make this cake!" I saw Carol at school one afternoon and told her about the wonderful recipe. She looked rather perplexed and told me she had never made a Raspberry Cream Cheese Coffee Cake, but it sounded delicious! That evening we both realized her mother had been talking about her good friend, Carol Witt, from All Seasons!

Breakfast

*K*aitlyn and Dell love this cake! It has a wonderful flavor with the spice cake and applesauce. The Maple Cream Cheese frosting adds an incredible richness to the cake. Good for breakfast or after a meal this is a wonderful cake to prepare ahead of time and serve at a brunch or coffee.

Oatmeal Spice Coffeecake

1¾	cups water divided
1	cup old fashion oats
1	(18.25-ounce) package spice cake mix
3	eggs
⅓	cup vegetable oil
1	cup applesauce
½	cup packed brown sugar

Preheat oven to 350°. Spray a bundt pan with nonstick cooking spray. Bring 1¼ cups of water to a boil then stir in oats. Set aside to cool for approximately 5 minutes. In a large mixing bowl, combine cake mix, eggs, oil, remaining ½ cup of water, applesauce, and brown sugar. Beat on low speed until blended, then beat for 2 minutes at medium speed. Stir in the oatmeal and beat an additional minute. Pour batter into prepared bundt pan. Bake for 40 minutes or until cake tests done. Cool 30 minutes in pan. Turn out on plate and ice with Maple Cream Cheese Frosting.

Note: This cake needs to be refrigerated to maintain its freshness. If you would like, set it out right before your guests arrive so it can reach room temperature. That way the icing will be creamy.

Maple Cream Cheese Frosting

½	stick butter, softened
1	(8-ounce) package of cream cheese, softened
¼	cup maple syrup
3¾	cups powdered sugar
2	tablespoons milk
1	teaspoon vanilla

Blend butter and cream cheese until smooth. Add syrup and mix well. Alternately add powered sugar and milk, beating after each addition. Add vanilla and beat until well blended and creamy.

Note: You can add a little more milk so the frosting is more like a glaze. This recipe makes a lot of frosting. You can freeze the leftover frosting and use it the next time you make this cake or any other spice cake.

To save time: Soften cream cheese in the microwave. Place in a microwave-safe bowl and heat at 50 % power for 20 to 30 seconds.

Breakfast

*T*he perfect compliment to the Oatmeal Spice Cake on the previous page. Actually, it would be good on any spice cake!

My friend is not perfect, no more than I, and so we suit each other admirably.

Breakfast

As I was testing recipes for this cookbook, I kept looking for a good basic coffee cake. I must have tested ten or more and then I remembered a recipe in my recipe collection. I had this cake at Terri Takes' home in Fort Worth. Her mom served this delicious cake and kindly shared the recipe with me years ago! Terri and I were Kappa pledges together at Texas Tech. Terri is a sweet friend, and we still keep in touch. She is married and the mother of five wonderful children!

Sour Cream Coffee Cake

¼	cup firmly packed brown sugar
2	teaspoons cinnamon
1	cup chopped pecans divided
1	(18.25-ounce) package yellow cake mix
¾	cup vegetable oil
½	cup sugar
1	cup sour cream
1	teaspoon vanilla
4	eggs

Preheat oven to 325°. Grease and flour a bundt cake pan. Combine brown sugar, cinnamon, and ½ cup pecans; set aside. Combine cake mix, vegetable oil, sugar, vanilla, and eggs; beat exactly 2 minutes at medium speed. Stir in remaining ½ cup of pecans. Pour ½ of batter into prepared pan; sprinkle brown sugar mixture over batter. Pour in remaining batter. Bake for 50 to 60 minutes until golden brown and cake begins to pull away from edge of pan. Cool for 30 minutes before turning out.

Note: This cake is so delicious by itself, it doesn't need a glaze!

Logan's Favorite Cinnamon Cake

2	cups all-purpose flour
2	teaspoons baking powder
½	teaspoon salt
1	cup sugar
6	tablespoons vegetable oil
¾	cup milk
1	egg
1	teaspoon vanilla

Topping:

¼	cup butter, melted
¼	cup flour
¾	cup sugar
1	tablespoon cinnamon

In mixing bowl, combine all ingredients except topping ingredients. Beat for 3 minutes. Batter should be light and fluffy. Pour into an 8x8-inch glass baking dish that has been sprayed with nonstick cooking spray. Mix together topping ingredients and spoon over batter. Take a knife and marble topping into the batter. Bake at 350° for 30 to 40 minutes or until toothpick comes out clean. Cut into squares and serve warm.

Yield: 8 servings

Breakfast

This is my son, Logan's, favorite breakfast cake! He likes the rich sugar and cinnamon topping. It can serve up to eight, but if you are serving teenagers count on serving four!

This cake is also great with coffee. It is very rich so it could be served in small slices at a coffee or brunch.

Practice hospitality.

Romans 12:13

Breakfast

As I traveled this past year promoting my first cookbook "Where Hearts Gather", I have made several new friends! I met JoAnne Bruner at the Country Peddler Show in Arlington, Texas. JoAnne and her husband were so kind to stop by the next time I was there and bring me this delicious muffin recipe! It is quick and easy. JoAnne cooks often for her church and has made dozens of these!

Sausage Cheese Muffins

1	pound hot pork sausage
1	(10¾-ounce) can Cheddar cheese soup (undiluted)
½	cup milk
2-3	teaspoons rubbed sage
3	cups biscuit baking mix

Preheat oven to 400°. Spray mini muffin pans with non-stick cooking spray. Cook sausage over medium heat until no longer pink; drain well. In a medium bowl, combine soup, milk, sage, and cooked sausage. Add biscuit mix and stir just until moistened. Fill greased mini muffin pans ⅔ full. Bake for 15 to 20 minutes. Serve warm.

Yield: 36 mini-muffins

Note: JoAnn likes to add onions & green chilies. Be sure to drain the green chilies really well or your muffins will be soggy.

These are especially good warm just out of the oven!

Applesauce Spiced Muffins

1	cup margarine, softened
2	cups sugar
2	eggs
2	cups applesauce
4	cups all-purpose flour
2	teaspoons baking soda
1	teaspoon salt
1	tablespoon cinnamon
2	tablespoons ground allspice
½	teaspoon ground cloves
1	cup finely chopped pecans

powdered sugar (optional)

Preheat oven to 350°. Spray mini muffin pans with non-stick cooking spray. Cream margarine and gradually add 2 cups sugar, beating well, at medium speed. Add eggs, one at a time, then add applesauce. Mix well. Combine flour and next five ingredients. Add to creamed mixture. Mix well and stir in pecans. Fill greased mini muffin cups about ¾ full. Bake for 14 minutes or until done. Cool on wire rack. Sift powdered sugar on top. (Just a light dusting of powdered sugar makes them extra pretty and tastes great too!)

Yield: 7 dozen mini muffins

Note: This batter will keep for about 2 weeks in the refrigerator, so you can have fresh hot muffins several mornings.

Breakfast

*A*nother wonderful recipe from All Seasons. This delicious recipe comes from Charlene McCann. These little muffins are packed with flavor. You can make them ahead of time and freeze, or since the batter keeps in the refrigerator enjoy hot muffins several mornings a week!

One of life's greatest treasures is the love that binds hearts together in friendship.

Breakfast

The name says it all...these are as rich and yummy as a pecan pie.

Pecans are popular in Texas, after all, it is our state tree! Plus many of us grew up with pecan trees in our backyards. My grandparents, Durward and Mary West, had several pecan trees around their house. As a child I did not like picking up all of the pecans! But, as an adult, I wish I had those big, old pecan trees around my house!

Pecan Pie Muffins

1	cup light brown sugar, packed
1	cup all-purpose flour
1½	cups chopped pecans
⅔	cup butter, softened
2	eggs

Preheat oven to 350°. Grease and flour mini muffin pans. In a medium bowl, stir together brown sugar, flour, and pecans. In a separate bowl, beat the butter and eggs together until smooth. Add dry ingredients and stir just until combined. Spoon the batter into prepared muffin cups. Fill ⅔ full. Sprinkle additional chopped pecans on top. Bake for 12 to 15 minutes. Cool on wire rack.

Yield: 36 mini muffins

Note: You can make these ahead of time and freeze them.

Orange Almond French Toast

¼	cup butter
⅓	cup brown sugar
¼	teaspoon cinnamon
1-2	teaspoons grated orange zest
⅓	cup sliced almonds
4	eggs, slightly beaten
⅔	cup orange juice
8	thick slices French bread

In a preheated 350° oven, melt butter in a jellyroll pan. Crumble brown sugar over melted butter. Sprinkle almonds, cinnamon and orange zest over sugar. Combine eggs and orange juice, mix thoroughly. Dip bread in egg mixture and allow it to soak up some of the liquid but don't let it get soggy. Arrange bread on pan and bake for 20 minutes. Serve almond side up with warm maple syrup.

Yield: 8 pieces

Note: It is best when prepared with french bread. You can substitute Texas-size toast, but it is not as good.

My family loves French toast, and yet I rarely have time to make it. We were all delighted to discover this recipe. It is quick and easy, as well as, being incredibly good! The perfect dish to serve overnight guests or for a special family breakfast.

Joy is not in things, it is in us.

Breakfast

J oni Jones and her husband stopped by my both at the Country Peddler Show in Amarillo. We began visiting and sharing stories about our love for cooking. They are very involved in their church and enjoy sharing their hospitality. When Joni told me she even made her own syrup I told her I had to have the recipe. She assured me it was easy. She was right!

Homemade Syrup

1	cup sugar
1	heaping tablespoon cornstarch
1½	cups water
2	teaspoons maple flavoring
3	tablespoons butter

Combine first 3 ingredients in a medium sauce pan. Bring to a boil over medium-high heat. As soon as mixture comes to a boil, remove from heat, and stir in maple flavoring and butter. Serve hot on french toast, pancakes, or anything calling for hot maple syrup.

Variations:
Add ½ teaspoon vanilla and ½ teaspoon of ground cinnamon. Yum! Be creative and try other flavorings.

The best and most beautiful things in the world cannot be seen or even touched. They must be felt with the heart.

Helen Keller

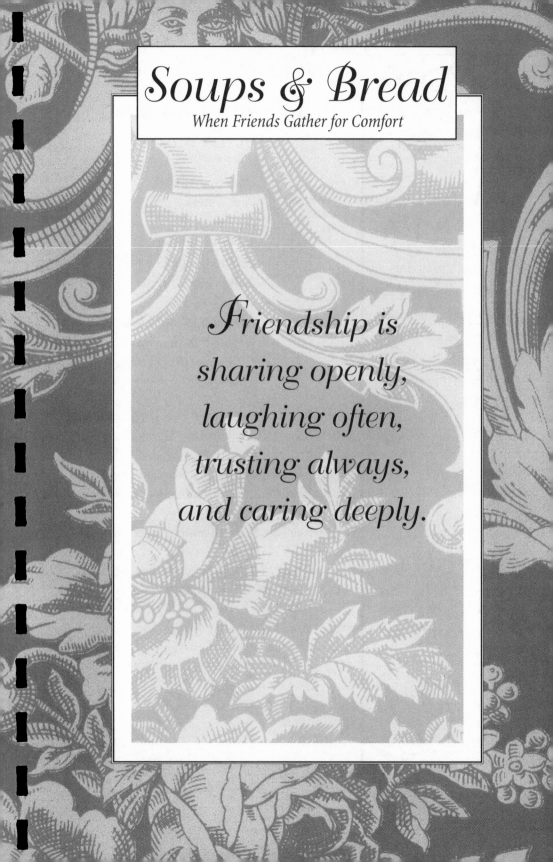

Soups & Bread
When Friends Gather for Comfort

*Friendship is
sharing openly,
laughing often,
trusting always,
and caring deeply.*

*W*e all have days when nothing is going right, or we just don't feel good. These are days when we need the comfort of Homemade Chicken Noodle Soup. The aroma will fill your kitchen, and before you know it you will begin to feel better!

Friendship is a cozy shelter from life's rainy days.

Homemade Chicken Noodle Soup

6	chicken breasts
10	cups water
2	teaspoons salt
1	teaspoon pepper
¾	onion, chopped
5	stalks celery, sliced
5	carrots, sliced
2	teaspoons poultry seasoning
1	teaspoon basil leaves
1	(12-ounce) package egg noodles

In a large stockpot, bring water, salt, pepper, and chicken to a boil. Reduce heat and simmer 30 minutes or until chicken is done. Remove chicken, reserving broth. Remove skin and bone from chicken. Chop chicken into bite-size pieces and return to broth. Add onion, celery, carrots, and seasonings. Bring to a boil; reduce heat and simmer for 45 minutes, stirring occasionally. Add noodles, stir, and heat 6 to 8 minutes or until noodles are tender. Adjust seasonings to taste.

Note: You can use boneless skinless chicken breasts, but cooking them with the skin and bone really does add a lot of flavor to the soup!

Baked Potato Soup

7	large baking potatoes, peeled, cubed, and cooked
⅔	cup butter
⅔	cup flour
7	cups whole milk
4	green onions, sliced
12	strips of bacon, cooked and crumbled
1¼	cups shredded Cheddar cheese
1¼	teaspoons salt
¾	teaspoon pepper
1	cup sour cream (optional)

In a saucepan, cook cubed potatoes until tender. Drain and set aside. In a large kettle or dutch oven, melt butter over medium heat. Stir in flour; continue to heat stirring until smooth. Gradually add milk, stirring constantly until thickened. Add cooked potatoes, onion, bacon, salt, and pepper. Reduce heat and simmer 10 minutes. Add cheese and stir until melted. If using the sour cream, add just before serving. Serve immediately.

Yield: 8 to 10 servings

A wonderful soup! This delicious recipe came to us from Sandi Mercier, a dear friend of my cousin, Donna Bradley. Sandi's mom enjoyed serving this at her annual ornament exchange. Sandi recently lost her mother. She told us "Whenever I make his soup, I'm filled with what Mom and I would call Gold Medal Memories."

A friend listens to our words, but hears our heart.

51

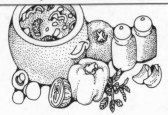

My first "real job" out of college was as an Interior Designer and Buyer at Hollon's Home Furnishings in Lubbock. Ken Wheatley was the store manager. This recipe is from his wife, Karen, and has been in my recipe file for many years. I loved working there. Jim and Donna Hollon and Ken and Karen watched me "grow up," fall in love, and get married. Their children were babies then. Today I have teenagers and some of their children are married! Now you know that I have had this delicious soup recipe for a very long time!!!

Canadian Cheese Soup

½	cup butter
¾	cup onion, finely diced
½	cup diced carrots
½	cup diced celery
½	cup flour
2	tablespoons cornstarch
1	quart (4 cups) chicken stock
1	quart (4 cups) milk
⅛	teaspoon soda
1	cup grated Cheddar cheese

salt and pepper to taste
chopped parsley for garnish

Melt butter in a large stockpot. Add onions, carrots, and celery; saute until tender. Blend in flour and cornstarch, stirring well. Add chicken stock and milk. Cook on medium heat, stirring constantly, until mixture has a smooth velvet texture and begins to thicken. Add soda and cheese; stir until blended. Season with salt and pepper. Garnish with parsley just before serving.

Yield: 10 servings

Note from Karen: If you use 2 ½ cups of cheese the soup is even better.

Cream Cheese Tomato Soup

2	tablespoons butter, melted
½	cup finely diced onion
6	ounces cream cheese, softened
2	(8-ounce) cans tomato soup
3	cups milk
2	(14-ounce) cans diced tomatoes
2	teaspoons basil
1	tablespoon fresh parsley, chopped

Melt butter in a medium saucepan; saute onions until tender (approximately 3 to 5 minutes). Reduce heat and add cream cheese, stirring until it melts. (Note: Adjust the heat if necessary you do not want this mixture to burn!) Add the tomato soup, stirring until smooth. Remove from heat and slowly add the milk, stirring until well blended. Return to heat and continue cooking. Add the diced tomatoes (juice and all) and the basil. Stir and continue heating until hot. Add parsley or sprinkle on top of each bowl as served.

Yield: 8 servings

My mom brought this wonderful recipe back from Minnesota after visiting her good friend Elaine Herron. Mom has known Elaine since they first met at the University of Texas. Later after they each married, my parents were visiting a new couple from their church. When the couple opened the door Mom and Elaine recognized each other! The couples became friends and attended the same Sunday School Class for years. I was named after Elaine. Even though distance has separated them over the years their friendship has remained just as close.

This mild soup is really good. It is easy to make and the perfect meal to serve to family and friends on a cold winter day. If your family likes things spicy add a can of diced tomatoes and green chilies.

Serving suggestion: For fun use red bandanas for napkins. Line a basket with a bandana and fill with fresh hot cornbread sticks.

When friends gather hearts are warmed.

Cowboy Stew

1½	pounds ground meat
2	tablespoons butter
1	bell pepper, chopped
1	onion, chopped
1	clove garlic, minced
1	(15-ounce) can tomato sauce
1	(15-ounce) can corn
1	(16-ounce) can pinto beans
4	cups cubed potatoes
1	tablespoon chili powder
2	cups water
2	teaspoons salt

fresh ground pepper to taste

In a large pot, brown ground meat. Drain well. Sauté pepper, onion, and garlic in butter until tender. Add to ground meat and stir. Add remaining ingredients. Stir until well combined. Simmer for 1 hour.

Yield: 8 servings

Serving Suggestion: Top with grated Cheddar cheese and serve with cornbread.

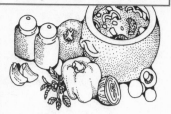

White Chicken Chili

2½	cups water
1	teaspoon lemon pepper
1	teaspoon cumin seed
4	boneless, skinless chicken breast halves
1	clove garlic, chopped
1	cup chopped onion
2	(8-ounce) cans white shoepeg corn, drained
2	(4-ounce) cans chopped green chilies
2-3	tablespoons lime juice
2	(14-ounce) cans white or great Northern beans, undrained
1	teaspoon sugar
1	tablespoon Worcestershire sauce

crushed tortilla chips, shredded fat-free Monterey Jack cheese for garnish

In a large saucepan, combine water with lemon pepper and cumin seed. Bring to a boil. Add the chicken breast halves and return to a boil. Reduce heat to low and simmer 20 minutes or until chicken is fork-tender and the juices run clear. Cut chicken into small pieces. Spray a medium skillet with nonstick cooking spray; add the garlic and onion. Cook, stirring, over low heat until tender. Add the chicken, onion/garlic mixture, corn, chilies, and lime juice to the broth. Bring to a boil Add beans, sugar, and Worcestershire; simmer 30 to 45 minutes.

Yield: 6 servings

A wonderful thick Southwestern soup from Eva Dean Stephens of Farwell, Texas. Eva Dean is a wonderful cook. We met her through her daughter, Kendra Head. Kendra was our son Logan's favorite teacher. You may remember her from our first cookbook. She and her husband, Darren, are part of the "famous" brownie story!

To serve: Place a small amount of tortilla chips and cheese in the bottom of each soup bowl. Ladle hot chili over chips and cheese. Serve with salsa. Enjoy!

*T*hroughout this cookbook you will find several recipes from Llwlyn Walker. She has been a friend of our family for many years. Her husband played football at Texas Tech with my uncle, Dwayne West. Later her daughter Vickie and I were both Kappas at Texas Tech!

We can do no great things, only small things with great love.

Santa Fe Soup

1½	pounds ground beef
1	onion, chopped
3	(10 ¾-ounce) cans Minestrone soup
1	(11-ounce) can corn
1	(14.5-ounce) can diced tomatoes
1	(10-ounce) can tomatoes and green chilies
1	(16-ounce) can Ranch-style beans

Brown ground meat and onion. Drain well. Add remaining ingredients. Stir well. Simmer at least one hour after bringing to a boil.

Yield: 10 generous helpings with "seconds" or 20 single servings.

Serving suggestion: Top with grated Cheddar cheese. Serve with warm cornbread. See next page for Llwlyn's favorite cornbread recipe.

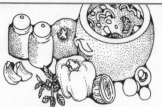

Llwlyn's Cornbread

1	cup white cornmeal
½	cup flour
3	teaspoons baking powder
1	teaspoon salt
2	tablespoons sugar
1	cup milk
1	egg, slightly beaten
2	tablespoons oil

Preheat oven and oiled cast-iron baking pan to 475°. In a medium-size bowl, mix together dry ingredients. Add milk, egg, and oil. Pour batter into hot, oiled, cornbread skillet, iron pan, or 8 x 8-inch glass dish. Bake at 475° for 15 to 20 minutes.

Note from Llwlyn: Heating the pan makes the cornbread crusty and really good.

This recipe uses the traditional white cornmeal. If you prefer you can substitute yellow cornmeal.

Llwlyn suggests using a cornbread skillet. This way each piece is good and crusty. The men in her house always wanted the corner piece until one of them gave her a divided cornbread skillet. Now they are all happy!

Kind words can be short and easy to speak, but their echoes are endless.

*W*ho would have thought that something so simple could be *soooo* good?! My family loves these little corn biscuits.

*A*nother quick and easy biscuit. This one is great to serve with a salad or meal.

Note: The California-style garlic powder is available at your local grocery store in the spice section.

Savory Cream Corn Biscuits

½	stick butter
1½	cups baking mix
1	(8-ounce) can cream-style corn

Preheat oven to 400°. Melt butter in a jelly roll pan (cookie sheet with sides). Stir together baking mix and corn. (Note: It will be thick and sticky!) Drop heaping teaspoons of dough onto pan. Roll in melted butter. Bake at 400° for 15 to 20 minutes or until golden brown. Serve hot.

Yield: 18 biscuits

Note: Add a dash of cayenne pepper for a little spice!

Cheese Garlic Biscuits

2	cups baking mix
⅔	cup milk
½	cup grated Cheddar cheese
¼	cup butter, melted
¼	teaspoon California-style garlic powder

Mix baking mix, milk, and cheese until a soft dough forms. Beat vigorously for 30 seconds. Drop dough by spoonfuls onto a lightly greased baking sheet. Bake at 450° for 15 minutes or until golden brown. Mix margarine and garlic powder together; brush on hot biscuits while they are still on the baking sheet. Serve warm.

Sesame Bread

1	package dry yeast
1¼	cups warm water
⅓	cup sugar
3½	cups flour
1	teaspoon salt
2	eggs
½	cup butter, softened
½	cup butter, melted
⅓	cup sesame seeds

Combine yeast, warm water, and sugar; stir and set aside. In a large bowl, combine flour and salt, add yeast mixture, eggs, and softened butter. Blend thoroughly and pour into a well greased bowl. Let rise covered about one hour. Stir down and pour into a well greased 9 x 13-inch pan. Pour melted butter on top and sprinkle with sesame seeds. Let rise 45 minutes to 1 hour. Bake at 400° for 25 to 30 minutes or until lightly brown. Cut into squares and serve.

Pam McPherson serves this scrumptious bread often, and I told her I had to have the recipe! The recipe actually is from her mother, Martha Fikes, and her good friend Mary Shannon of Ft. Worth. Mary does catering and created this delicious bread after tasting a similar bread made by a local chef.

When hands reach out in friendship, hearts are touched with joy.

*ich and delicious
these little biscuits will
melt in your mouth.
They are especially
good with soup or a
salad.*

Cream Cheese Biscuits

12	ounces cream cheese, softened
1	cup butter, softened
1½	cups all-purpose flour
1½	teaspoons baking powder
1	teaspoon salt

Mix cream cheese and butter together until smooth. Combine dry ingredients and gradually blend into cream cheese/butter mixture (you may have to use your hands). Divide dough into 6 portions and refrigerate for at least 30 minutes. On a lightly floured work surface, roll out one portion at a time; to approximately ¼-inch thickness. Cut out bite-size biscuits using a 1-inch to 1¼-inch biscuit cutter. Place 1-inch apart on ungreased baking sheet. Bake at 425° for 10 to 12 minutes or until light brown. Cool on wire racks.

Yield: 48 biscuits

*A friend is
one who
believes
in you when
you have
ceased to
believe
in yourself.*

Savory Cheese Loaf

1	large loaf of French bread
2	sticks butter, melted
2	tablespoons prepared mustard
½	cup minced onion
2	tablespoons poppy seed
1	pound Swiss cheese, sliced
10	slices bacon, cooked crisp and crumbled

Make a foil tray that is little longer and wider than the loaf of bread. Set tray aside. Slice a thin layer off top of bread. Slice bread loaf into serving sizes, but do not cut completely through loaf (so it will stay together).Set loaf on foil tray. In a saucepan, melt butter; add mustard, onion, poppy seed and ⅔ of bacon crumbles. Stir until well blended and remove from heat. Put a piece of cheese between each slice of bread. Spoon butter mixture between slices. Pour leftover mixture on top of bread. Sprinkle with remaining bacon. Bake at 400° until cheese is melted and top is lightly brown.

Helpful Hint: Slide foil tray on to a cookie sheet. This will make it easier to remove the hot loaf from the oven.

Note: Martha said you can prepare this bread ahead of time and freeze it.

*M*artha McCormick sent in this wonderful bread recipe! Martha is a delightful person and a dear friend of my family. She is the Travel Coordinator for one of the Keller banks and my parents enjoyed several trips with her. She and my mother have shared many joys and sorrows. They often take turns treating each other to lunch so they can "check on" each other. Martha said this bread was a favorite of her dad's. She also said it is great to serve for picnics and barbeques.

Sally Cabel teaches 2nd grade with my sister, Karen, in Edmond, Oklahoma. This recipe provides a delightful change of pace from your ordinary ham and cheese sandwich!

I love homemade Pimento Cheese! Try using half Sharp cheese and half mild Cheddar. Spread on lightly toasted wheat bread and enjoy! You can add a dash of cayenne or even diced jalapeños for a spicy version!

Hot Ham & Cheese Sandwiches

12	small rolls
1	pound shaved ham
12	slices Swiss or Pepper Jack cheese
½	cup margarine, melted
1½	tablespoons mustard
1½	teaspoons Worcestershire
1	teaspoon onion flakes

Assemble sandwiches with ham and cheese of your choice. Place on a baking sheet. Add mustard, worcestershire, and onion flakes to melted margarine. Pour over sandwiches. Bake for 20 minutes at 350°.

Homemade Pimento Cheese

1	(3-ounce) cream cheese, softened
4	cups grated Cheddar cheese
3	tablespoons mayonnaise
1	(2-ounce) jar pimentos, drained and mashed
⅛	teaspoon California-style garlic powder
⅛	teaspoon onion powder
fresh ground pepper to taste	

Using your mixer beat cream cheese and cheese until blended. Add remaining ingredients and beat until well mixed.

Herb Garden Bread

4½	cups all-purpose flour
2	tablespoons sugar
2	envelopes dry yeast
1	envelope Ranch-style dressing mix
½	teaspoon dried thyme leaves
1	teaspoon parsley flakes
1	teaspoon dried dill weed
1½	cups hot tap water
¼	cup diced fresh chives
1	cup cottage cheese
2	tablespoons olive oil
2	eggs, beaten
¾	cup Parmesan cheese
4	tablespoons melted butter

In a large bowl, combine dry ingredients. Stir in hot water. Add chives and cottage cheese. Stir until blended. Add oil, eggs, and Parmesan. Continue stirring, adding melted butter until all ingredients are well blended. (Note: dough will be soft and sticky). Cover and let rise until doubled. Punch down and divide into 2 loaf pans that have been well greased. Cover and let rise about 1 hour or until doubled. Preheat oven to 375°. Bake for 30 to 35 minutes or until golden brown. Let cool in pans for 10 minutes then remove and place on wire racks to cool completely.

Yield: 2 loaves

The herbs and cheeses give this bread a unique flavor. It does take a little more time to make, but the results are well worth it. Serve it warm with butter or use it to turn an ordinary sandwich into a gourmet delight!

Serve one another in love.
Galations 5:13

63

*M*y mom's dear
friend, Mary Wells,
is known for this
wonderful strawberry
bread. She has shared
it with many friends
through the years.
Recently she and my
mom gave a baby
shower for Edith
Shallene's daughter,
Stephanie. Since the
shower was around
lunchtime they served a
salad lunch in cute
baskets with this
strawberry bread on the
side. In the rectangular
baskets, they placed a
pretty napkin liner and
three clear punch-size
plastic cups. Each cup
was filled with a
different salad. Chicken,
green, and fruit salads
were used. This bread
served as the dessert!

Mary's Strawberry Bread

2	cups flour
½	cup sugar
¾	teaspoon baking powder
¼	teaspoon salt
1	(3-ounce) package strawberry jello
⅔	cup chopped pecans
1	egg, beaten
3	tablespoons margarine, melted
1	teaspoon vanilla
¾	teaspoon baking soda
1	(10-ounce) package frozen strawberries, thawed

Sift flour, sugar, baking powder, and salt together. Stir in jello and nuts. Combine egg, margarine, and vanilla. Add to dry ingredients. Mix soda with strawberries, add to mixture and blend thoroughly. Pour into small loaf pans or regular-size loaf pans that have been greased and floured. Bake at 350° until bread tests done. For small loaf pans cook about 30 minutes; for the large loaf cook approximately 1 hour.

Serve with butter or cream cheese.

Sweet Potato Bread

3	cups sugar
1	cup vegetable oil
⅔	cup water
4	eggs
2	teaspoons vanilla
1½	cups cooked and mashed sweet potatoes
3⅓	cups flour
1½	teaspoons salt
1	teaspoon baking soda
1	teaspoon cinnamon
1	teaspoon freshly ground nutmeg
1	cup chopped pecans

Preheat oven to 350°. Grease and flour 2, one pound loaf pans. In a large mixing bowl combine sugar, oil, water, eggs, vanilla and sweet potatoes. Stir until sugar is dissolved and blends with other ingredients. Combine dry ingredients and gradually stir into mixture. Add pecans. Mix until well blended. Pour into loaf pans and bake at 350° for 1 hour or until loaf tests done with a toothpick.

Yield: 2 loaves

Billie Jeane Garner sent us this delicious bread recipe. I have known Billie Jeane since I was in High School and played the piano at Keller Methodist Church. She was in the church choir and always was so kind and encouraging to me. Billie Jeane is a home economist and a wonderful cook! Billie Jeane, Jane Bryant, Peggy Payne, and Mary Richardson were the first ones to greet mom and me when we had our booksigning at the Barnes and Noble in Grapevine. We were nervous, and seeing these four special ladies helped calm our nerves. We knew we were not alone! They were the first of many good friends that stopped by to see us.

My dear friend, Liz Langford, shared this delightful recipe. It is from her mother-in-law, Daisy Langford, from Dimmitt, Texas. I loved it because it is quick and easy. Plus the addition of the cream cheese makes it incredibly yummy!

Note: 3 medium bananas will yield a little over one cup mashed. Also use ripe bananas, they have more flavor!

Daisy's Banana Nut Bread

1	cup sugar
1	(8-ounce) package cream cheese, softened
1	cup mashed bananas
2	eggs
2	cups biscuit mix
½	cup pecans, chopped

In a mixing bowl, cream together sugar and cream cheese until light and fluffy. Beat in bananas and eggs; add biscuit mix and pecans. Blend until dry ingredients are moist. Pour into a greased 9x5x3 loaf pan. Bake at 350° for 1 hour.

*A friend is a close companion
on rainy days,
someone to share with
through every phase...
Forgiving and helping to
bring out the best,
believing the good and
forgetting the rest.*

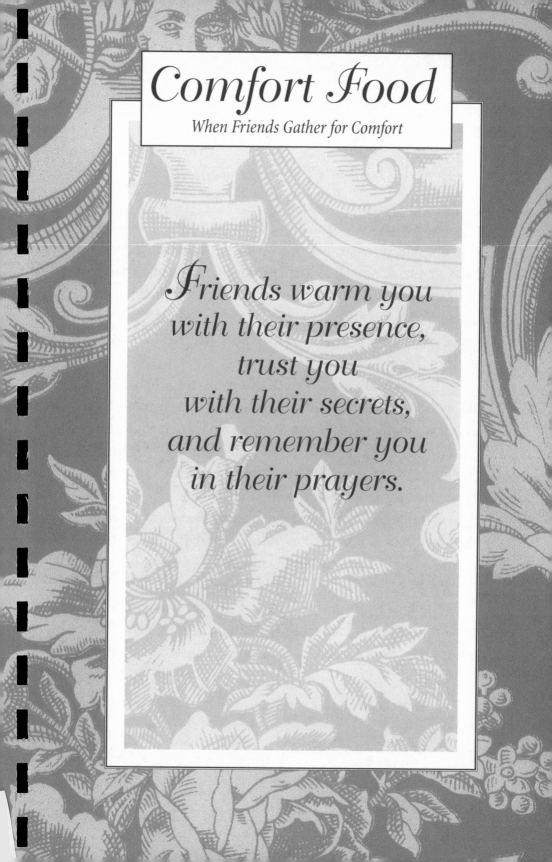

Comfort Food

When Friends Gather for Comfort

*Friends warm you
with their presence,
trust you
with their secrets,
and remember you
in their prayers.*

What is Comfort Food?

Some have described it as those particular foods we crave in times of crisis; like mashed potatoes, fried chicken, chocolate pie, or a bowl of homemade soup. Whichever food you crave there is usually a memory attached... something or someone that provides a warm comforting memory. Often the memory is one of having shared this particular food with family or friends.

It is not only the food, but this gathering with others that adds to the comfort. There is something healing and sustaining about sitting around a table and sharing a meal. Not only do we share food, but we share our lives. We gain strength and encouragement from each other and the knowledge that we will not face life alone.

We often share comfort food during the loss of a loved one. This ritual is part of our culture especially here in the South. The preparing and serving of food is a way of sharing in other's grief... of saying that we care and that we hurt too. On the following pages are some of our favorite comfort foods. We have also included thoughtful things to do when you are wondering "What can I do to help comfort my friend?"

Murfreesboro Fried Chicken

6-8   chicken pieces (bone in, skin on)
2-3   cups flour
salt and pepper to taste
1   cup buttermilk

Put flour, salt, and pepper in a brown paper bag. Pour buttermilk in a shallow bowl. Drop 2 to 3 pieces of chicken into bag and shake to coat with flour. Remove chicken and dip in buttermilk. Put chicken pieces back in bag and shake well to form a thick coating. Fry in hot oil (about 1-inch deep) in an electric skillet or on the stove top until golden brown. Turn and fry other side until brown. Remove chicken to a pan lined with newspaper or paper towels to cool and allow paper to soak up extra oil. Reserve the drippings to make gravy (see next page for recipe).

Note from Ginny: She likes to use garlic salt in the flour mixture.

If you like fried chicken with a crispy crust, this is a great recipe! Ginny Huddleston Secor shared this family favorite. She said it is often requested by family members including the grandchildren who want it for their "birthday meals"! Karen West Franks, (Ginny's college room-mate and my sister) gave this recipe the name Murfreesboro Fried Chicken because Ginny's parents grew up in Murfreesboro, Tennessee.

Comfort Food

*M*ashed potatoes are definitely part of the comfort food category. And if you are having Fried Chicken, you have to have mashed potatoes and cream gravy!

*T*he perfect compliment to mashed potatoes. Use the pan drippings and crispy bits too. They give it a great flavor!

Homemade Mashed Potatoes

3-4	baking potatoes, peeled and cut into chunks
1	stick butter
½	cup warm milk

Salt and fresh ground pepper

Cook potatoes in boiling salted water until fork-tender. Drain well. Add butter and mash with potato masher. Stir in milk and mix with potato masher or electric mixer. Season with salt and pepper. Whip until smooth and creamy. (Note: You can whip with a masher or whisk; you do not have to use a mixer.)

Cream Gravy

2	tablespoons pan drippings
¼	cup flour
2	cups milk

salt and pepper to taste

Drain pan drippings, reserving 2 tablespoons in skillet. Place skillet over low heat and add ¼ cup flour, stirring into drippings to make a paste. Cook about 1 minute; stirring constantly. Gradually add milk; cook over medium heat. Continue to stir constantly and cook until gravy has thickened and is bubbly. Add ½ teaspoon salt and pepper. Adjust seasonings to taste. Serve over potatoes.

Grandmother's Baked Squash

2	pounds yellow squash, sliced
½	onion, chopped
¼	cup sour cream
	salt and pepper to taste

Boil squash and onion together until tender. Drain well. Mash squash with potato masher; drain again. Stir in sour cream; season to taste. Place in a 1½-quart covered casserole dish that has been sprayed with nonstick cooking spray. Bake at 350° for 20 minutes; uncover and bake 10 more minutes.

Fresh Green Beans

2	pounds fresh green beans, washed, ends removed, and snapped into 2-inch pieces
3	slices of uncooked bacon, diced
2	tablespoons butter
1	teaspoon sugar
2	teaspoons salt

Cook bacon in saucepan until tender, but not crisp. Remove from heat and add beans. Pour in just enough water to cover. Add butter, sugar, and salt. Place saucepan back on burner and bring to a boil. Reduce heat and cook until tender.

Comfort Food

An old-fashioned favorite. My mother-in-law, Naydiene, said this was the way her mother cooked squash. It is simple to make and has a wonderful flavor. This is a repeat from our first cookbook, but it is one of those comfort foods I often crave!

This is also from "Where Hearts Gather," but is worth repeating. Green Beans just go with Fried Chicken and Homemade Mashed Potatoes! I always look forward to summer when fresh beans are available.

Comfort Food

Another classic comfort food. This mild favorite is just the thing to warm you when it's cold outside or for those days when you're feeling blue.

While great talent and intellect are to be admired, they cannot dry one tear or mend a broken spirit. Only kindness can do this.

Old-Fashion Chicken Spaghetti

4	chicken breasts, cooked and cut into bite-size pieces
1	(8-ounce) package spaghetti
1	onion, chopped
1	green pepper, chopped
1	stick margarine or butter
¾	cup flour
4	cups milk
2	cups grated sharp Cheddar cheese
⅛	teaspoon cayenne pepper
⅛	teaspoon California-style garlic powder
	salt and pepper

Boil spaghetti in chicken broth. Sauté onion and green pepper in 1 tablespoon butter until tender. Place sauteed vegetables, cooked spaghetti, and cut up chicken in a large bowl. Make a white sauce by melting 1 stick of butter in a saucepan. Stir in flour to make a paste. Gradually add milk, stirring until smooth. Cook over medium-low heat until mixture begins to thicken. Add cheese and stir until melted and cheese is well blended into sauce. Add cayenne and garlic powder. Pour over chicken mixture and stir until blended. Place in a large baking dish that has been sprayed with nonstick cooking spray. Bake at 350° for 20 to 30 minutes or until bubbly. Top with additional grated cheese if desired.

Homemade Macaroni & Cheese

1	(8-ounce) package elbow macaroni
2	tablespoons butter
2	tablespoons flour
1	teaspoon salt
1	teaspoon dry mustard
2	cups shredded sharp Cheddar cheese
2½	cups milk
¼	cup buttered bread crumbs

paprika for garnish

Prepare macaroni according to package directions. While it is cooking, melt butter in a medium saucepan over low heat. Remove from heat and blend in flour, salt, and mustard. Return to heat and gradually stir in milk. Heat over medium heat stirring until sauce is smooth and thick. Add 1½ cups of cheese; stir until it melts. Drain macaroni and add to cheese sauce. Pour into a 2-quart casserole that has been sprayed with nonstick cooking spray. Top with remaining cheese, bread crumbs, and paprika. Bake at 375° for 20 to 25 minutes until bubbly.

The ultimate comfort food. I can eat this by the bowlful. Who needs anything else? This is a meal in itself! Val Franks brought a large dish of her wonderful macaroni and cheese when my Dad passed away. Not only was her thoughtfulness greatly appreciated, but my sister, Karen, and I were pleased because Val's macaroni and cheese is one of our favorites!

*P*eggy Allen from Abilene, Texas, sent in this wonderful recipe. Peggy prepared this casserole for a family meal that was served after a funeral. One lady told Peggy it was better than the desserts!

A friend is one who joyfully sings with you when you are on the mountaintop, and silently walks with you through the valley.

Calico Corn Casserole

4	tablespoons butter
1	medium bell pepper, chopped
1	medium onion, chopped
2	(11-ounce) cans cream-style corn
2	eggs, beaten
2	teaspoons sugar
1	cup uncooked Minute rice
1	(4-ounce) jar diced pimentos, drained
salt and pepper to taste	
1	cup grated Cheddar cheese

In a large saucepan, sauté bell pepper and onion in butter until tender. Remove from heat and add corn, eggs, and sugar. Add rice and pimentos; stir until well blended. Season with salt and pepper. Pour in a 9x13-inch baking dish that has been sprayed with nonstick cooking spray. Bake for 25 to 30 minutes at 350˚. Top with 1 cup Cheddar cheese and bake until cheese melts.

Mom's Homemade Rolls

2	packages yeast
2	cups lukewarm water
½	cup sugar
½	cup shortening
2	tablespoons salt
2	eggs
6	cups flour, unsifted

Dissolve yeast in water and set aside. With your mixer, cream shortening, sugar and salt. Add eggs and mix well. Alternately add yeast-water mixture and flour. Turn dough out onto a floured surface and knead until it gets stiff. Place dough in refrigerator for several hours or overnight. Make into rolls (Mom just pats the dough into rounded rolls; the size depends on how many she needs and what she is serving them with). Let rise for 30 minutes to 1 hour. Bake in a preheated 350° oven for 15 to 20 minutes.

Yield: 24 rolls

Note: Mom says, you do not have to refrigerate dough. Let rise in the bowl; punch down and then make into rolls. Let rolls rise, then follow instructions for baking.

These rolls freeze well. Mom often makes the rolls ahead of time and cooks them until they are done but just lightly brown. Then freezes them in the pan, thaws them at room temperature and reheats the rolls before the meal.

Comfort Food

My mom, Jeanette West, is known for her rolls. In our first cookbook we called them Grammy Rolls. The recipe actually came from my grandmother, Eunice Owen, my mother's mother. But the grand kids now call them Grammy Rolls after my mom. The rolls are great to take to someone because they work with a meal or are wonderful toasted with butter for breakfast. See next page for Mom's wonderful Cinnamon Rolls made from this recipe.

Mom often takes her homemade cinnamon rolls to help comfort others. We sometimes forget, but one of the things a family in crisis or during the loss of a loved one needs is something to feed everyone for breakfast!

God does not comfort us to make us comfortable, but to help us comfort others.

Grammy's Homemade Cinnamon Rolls

4	tablespoons butter, softened
¼	cup brown sugar
⅛	cup sugar
2	teaspoons cinnamon

Make dough using mom's homemade roll recipe. (see previous page) Let rise in bowl. Punch down; place dough on floured work surface and press into large rectangle. Spread softened butter on rectangle leaving ½-inch around the edge. Sprinkle with brown sugar, white sugar and cinnamon. Starting with long edge, roll up and pinch seams to seal. Slice into 1½-inch sections. Place in a 9x13-inch baking dish that has been sprayed with nonstick cooking spray. Let rise. Bake at 350° for 20 to 25 minutes until golden brown. Drizzle glaze over warm rolls and serve.

Glaze:

1	cup powdered sugar
½	teaspoon vanilla
1½ - 2½	teaspoons milk

Combine all ingredients and stir until smooth.

Note: After placing rolls in pan, you can cover them and refrigerate overnight or freeze up to a month. If frozen, allow rolls to thaw at room temperature then let rise in a warm oven before baking.

Nona's Best Buttermilk Pound Cake

1	cup shortening
2	cups sugar
3	eggs
2	cups flour
½	teaspoon soda
⅛	teaspoon salt
1	teaspoon baking powder
1	cup buttermilk
1	tablespoon vanilla
1	tablespoon almond extract

Cream shortening and sugar, add eggs and beat well. Sift together, flour, soda, salt, and baking powder. Add dry ingredients to egg mixture, alternating with buttermilk. Mix in extracts. Pour into a tube pan that has been greased and floured then bake in a 350° oven for 30 minutes. Turn down oven to 300° and bake an additional 30 minutes. (Note: Do not open oven door until the cake has cooked at least 50 minutes or your cake may fall. I speak from experience!) Cool and remove from pan.

Comfort Food

*M*y cousin, Donna Bradley, sent me this wonderful pound cake recipe. She said it was easy and that she often took it to friends. It is also special because the recipe belonged to her grandmother, Mildred Barney, better known to all of us as "Nona".

Silences make the real conversations between friends. Not the saying, but the never needing to say is what counts.

Comfort Food

*A*nn Brian shared this delicious pound cake recipe. She told us that a cousin brought the cake to her house after a funeral. Ann said it looked like just another pound cake and sat on her counter for a couple of days. Wow, was she surprised when she cut into it! This cake was wonderful!

Note: Ann said, in order to achieve the same results do not substitute another brand of cake mix. Duncan Hines really does make the best cakes. I would have to agree!

Chocolate Chip Pound Cake

1	box Duncan Hines (yellow or white) cake mix
1	(3-ounce) box instant chocolate pudding
3	eggs
¾	cup oil
¾	cup water
1	(8-ounce) carton sour cream
1	cup mini chocolate chips

In mixing bowl, combine cake mix, pudding mix, eggs, oil, water, and sour cream. Beat for 4 minutes. Stir in chocolate chips. Bake in a greased and floured bundt pan at 350° for 55 to 60 minutes.

Note: This cake does not really need an icing, but the chocolate glaze on page 147 makes it an extra special chocolate treat!

What Can I Do?

If cooking or providing food is not your gift, try the following list of things you can bring or do:

Bring Paper Goods:
Hot and cold cups, large and small paper plates, napkins, plasticware, and paper towels

Kleenex and toilet paper is also appreciated.

Refrigerators get overloaded during funerals due to the abundance of food, so loaning the family an ice chest is a nice gesture. Even nicer is to bring an extra one and fill it with bags of ice or soft drinks.

Snack items are also a good idea. A basket of fruit, snack crackers, and small packages of cookies.

Easy to prepare breakfast items like muffins, yogurt, and small boxes of cereal.

Assorted coffees and teas.

Also offer to help answer the door and phone. Or offer to stay at the house while the family is away planning the funeral and then later during the service.

All of these were done for my family when my dad suddenly passed away. The out-pouring of love and food helped us through a very difficult time. Your thoughtfulness and love will be just as appreciated by someone else in need.

Comfort Food

*O*ther favorite comfort foods that are good to take to others:

Applesauce Cake (page 152)

Baked Potato Soup (page 51)

Buffalo Chip Cookies (page 171)

Chocolate Dream Cake (page 150)

Lemon Pound Cake (page 140)

Mrs. Adams Corn Casserole (page 123)

Oatmeal Crisps (page 177)

Poppy Seed Chicken and Rice Casserole (page 106)

Reba's Chocolate Pie (page 165)

Comfort Food

I had not heard this story until I was in College Station visiting with my friend Cissy Mobley (see story and recipe on page 159). Cissy shared the story with me. She felt like it really fit in with my stories about hospitality, and reminded me that not only does food nourish us physically, but also the time spent sharing food with others feeds our soul. A few months later at a Country Peddler Show, Homer Hollis (an exhibitor across the aisle from me) walked up to my booth and handed me a card with this story on it and a fork pin attached. I knew God was saying; "Share this story!"

Keep Your Fork

There was a woman who had been diagnosed with a terminal illness and had been given three months to live. So, she contacted her preacher to discuss her final wishes. She told him which songs she wanted sung, what scriptures she would like read, and what outfit she wanted to be buried in. The woman also requested to be buried with her Bible.

"There is one more thing," she said excitedly. "What is that?" asked the preacher. "I want to be buried with a fork in my right hand." The minister stood looking at the woman, not knowing what to say. "That surprises you, doesn't it?", asked the woman. "Well, to be honest yes." replied the preacher.

The woman went on to explain. "In all my years of attending those church potluck dinners, I always remember that when the dishes were being cleared, someone would always say, "Keep your fork...the best is yet to come!"

So the next time you reach down to pick up your fork; remember, by God's grace, the best is yet to come!

For the test of the heart is trouble, and it always comes with the years, And the smile that is worth the praises, Is the smile that shines through tears.

Salads

When Friends Gather for Fun

*The best in me
and the best in you.
Hailed each other
because they knew.
That always
and always
since life began.
Our being friends
was part of God's plan.*

Salads

*M*artha Birdwell shared this wonderful salad recipe with us. It is a beautiful salad, as well as a very tasty one. The Birdwells are some of our oldest and dearest friends. Our families have laughed together, cried together, and loved each other for many years.

A friend is a present you give yourself.

Fresh Garden Salad

1	package Italian green salad mix
1	package Spring green salad mix
1	(5-ounce) can black olives, cut in half
1	(14-ounce) can artichoke hearts, drained and cut into bite-size pieces
1	(14-ounce) can hearts of palm, drained and sliced
1	red pepper, cut into thin strips
1	bunch green onions, cut into small pieces, stems included
1	(3-ounce) package grated Parmesan cheese

In a large salad bowl, toss all ingredients together. Chill.

Dressing:

¾	cup good quality olive oil
	juice of ½ lime
½	teaspoon salt
¼	teaspoon pepper
½	teaspoon Italian herbs
¼	teaspoon garlic powder

Mix and toss into salad right before serving.

Juli's Favorite Spinach Salad

2	(10-ounce) packages of fresh spinach, stems removed and leaves torn into pieces
6	slices of bacon, cooked and crumbled
2	eggs, hard-boiled and chopped
2	cups fresh mushrooms, sliced
½	cup grated Swiss or Parmesan cheese
¼	package Pepperidge Farm herb stuffing

Dressing:

½	cup sugar
1	cup salad oil
½	cup green onions, sliced
1	teaspoon dry mustard
⅓	cup vinegar
½	teaspoon salt
½	teaspoon pepper
1	teaspoon celery seed

Mix together dressing ingredients until well blended. Set aside. This dressing tends to separate so you will need to whisk it again right before you pour it on salad. In a large salad bowl, combine spinach, bacon, chopped eggs, mushrooms, and cheese. Toss. Right before serving sprinkle on stuffing mix and pour on dressing. Note: This salad is not good leftover, so you only want to prepare the amount you need for that meal.

My dear friend, Juli McArthur, served this wonderful salad when we visited her home. She said it was her favorite, and after tasting it, I can see why! It is incredible! The stuffing mix adds a unique touch, and the dressing is a delicious blend of flavors. Juli and I have been good friends since we first met at Texas Tech. We were both Interior Design majors, and shared similar family backgrounds. We do not get to see each other often, but when we do it is just like no time has passed at all. Even our kids get along extremely well. Maybe some of them will attend Tech together!

83

Salads

Haughton Girls Party Salad

*J*ennie Haughton was my roommate at Texas Tech. I met her through my cousin, Donna,who was friends with Jennie's older sisters Ann and Louisa. After our first "potluck" roommates didn't work out, Jennie and I decided to try being roommates. We ended up staying roommates for over 4 years until each of us finished college at Tech! Jennie and her sisters often made this salad, and I have had it in my recipe collection since that time. It is still a favorite, as are the memories from those days at Tech with the Haughton sisters!

½	(10-ounce) package fresh spinach, stems removed and torn into pieces
6	hard-boiled eggs, sliced
½	pound ham, julienned
1	small head of iceberg lettuce, torn into bite-size pieces
1	red onion
1	cup sour cream
1	pint mayonnaise
2	cups Cheddar cheese
½	pound bacon, cooked crisp and crumbled

In bottom of a large glass salad bowl, spread the raw spinach. Add a layer of boiled eggs. Next a layer of ham and then a layer of iceberg lettuce.Sprinkle with salt and pepper. Separate the onion into rings and spread over lettuce. Mix sour cream and mayonnaise together and spread evenly on top. Sprinkle cheese on top. Cover with plastic wrap and refrigerate several hours. Just before serving sprinkle with bacon. Do <u>not</u> toss. Serve portions all the way to the bottom.

Zucchini Salad

3	medium zucchini, sliced thin
½	green pepper, sliced thin
½	onion, sliced thin
½	cup celery, thinly sliced

Marinade:

⅔	cup cider vinegar
½	cup sugar
⅓	cup salad oil
¼	cup burgundy cooking wine
2	tablespoons red wine vinegar
1	teaspoon salt
½	teaspoon pepper

Combine vegetables in an air-tight plastic bowl; set aside. Combine ingredients for marinade and pour over vegetables. Seal container and refrigerate for 12 hours.

Yield: 6 servings

Another wonderful salad from Martha Birdwell. This one was in Naydiene's recipe box and dated 1980. It is still a family favorite. Naydiene was always selective about the recipes she chose to put in her recipe box. If it was in there, you knew it had received a high rating from Naydiene! Martha is a wonderful cook and could fill her own cookbook with her delicious recipes!

A friend is someone who comes in when the whole world has gone out.

Salads

A pretty and delicious salad from Sue White and her daughter Kamber Carson Smith. We first met Kamber when she was a teenager. She is now married and the mother of a precious daughter named Kondi.

It is not how much we have, but how much we enjoy, that makes happiness.

Mandarin Orange Salad

½	cup salad oil
¼	cup vinegar
¼	cup sugar
2	teaspoons minced onion
½	teaspoon salt
⅛	teaspoon paprika
1	head of lettuce
1	(11-ounce) can Mandarin oranges, drained
1	(2.8-ounce) can fried onions
1	avocado, sliced

With a whisk, combine oil, vinegar, sugar, minced onion, salt and paprika together. Place lettuce and oranges in a large salad bowl. Right before serving, add the fried onions and sliced avocado on top. Pour dressing over and serve.

Note: I like to prepare and slice the avocado right before serving, so it is fresh and has not begun to turn brown.

Chicken Pasta Salad

1	bag tri-colored pasta spirals
3	chicken breasts, boiled and chopped into bite-size pieces
1	purple onion, chopped
1	bell pepper, chopped
2	stalks of celery, chopped
1	small can sliced black olives
1	cucumber, diced
1	jar Marie's Ranch-style dressing

salt and pepper to taste

Cook chicken. Remove from broth, cool, and cut into bite-size pieces. Add spirals to chicken broth and cook until done. (Note: You may need to add additional water). Rinse pasta under cold water until cool. Add remaining ingredients. Chill until ready to serve. Serve with round butter crackers or toasted wheat crackers. Make ahead of time so the flavors have time to blend. This salad keeps well in the refrigerator.

Serves: 6-8 generous portions

Note: You can find Marie's salad dressing in the refrigerated vegetable section at your local grocer. When putting salad dressing on, I like to add it gradually, stirring until the salad has the taste and consistency I like. Sometimes you may not want or need a whole jar of the dressing.

Each year Naomi Brown and Jeanne Novotny have the most wonderful seminar for decorative painters. The seminar is held in beautiful Eagles Nest, New Mexico, and is taught by Heidi Brown. Jeanne is also a gourmet cook. This recipe is from that seminar and was given to me by my cousin, Rosemary West. Rosemary said that everything that Naomi and Jeanne do for the seminar is lovely, from the centerpieces to the food. Even the door prizes are special. At the seminar, they served this salad with fruit, yeast rolls, and a dessert.

Laneta Watson, is a dear friend of my cousin, Rosemary West. They met when she and her husband Bob were students at Texas Wesleyan University in Fort Worth. They are now both retired teachers living in New Braunfels, Texas. Laneta and Rosemary have remained friends and enjoy visiting each others homes several times a year. Laneta loves to cook, and she and Rosemary enjoy exchanging recipes. This salad is one of those delicious "exchanges"!

Broccoli Salad

1	head of broccoli, cut into bite-size pieces
1	small onion, chopped
1	cup raisins
1	cup sunflower seeds
10-12	slices bacon cooked crisp and crumbled
1	cup mayonnaise
2	tablespoons vinegar
½	cup sugar

Wash broccoli and drain well. Cut off florets and set aside stems. Cut florets and tender part of stem into bite-size pieces. Combine with onion, raisins, sunflower seeds, and bacon. In a small bowl, combine the mayonnaise, vinegar, and sugar until well blended. Pour over broccoli mixture and stir lightly. Cover and refrigerate until well chilled.

All Seasons' Pasta Salad

1	(16-ounce) package three color, spiral pasta cooked as directed and drained
1	large cucumber, half slices
3	Roma tomatoes, diced
1	green bell pepper, diced
3	green onions, diced
1	link smoked sausage, sliced
1	(8-ounce) block medium Cheddar cheese, cut into small cubes

Combine all ingredients in a large bowl. Pour on dressing, toss and chill overnight.

Dressing:

¾	cup canola oil
1½	cups vinegar
2	teaspoons dry mustard
1	teaspoon pepper
1	teaspoon accent
2	tablespoons parsley flakes
1	teaspoon garlic salt
1	cup sugar

Mix all ingredients, heat and stir until sugar is dissolved. Cool slightly and pour over pasta mixture.

Sue Ellen Bumpus sent in this delicious salad. It is her version of a salad served during painting classes at All Seasons. Sue Ellen added the sausage and cheese. She says it is more "manly" that way. Which means her husband enjoys it! She said they enjoy the salad year round, but especially in the summer. You can serve the salad with or without the additions. Either way, it is a great luncheon salad.

*A*nother favorite from All Seasons. This has been a part of their recipe collection for so long no one remembers for sure who first brought it! Many credit Sherry Brandt, who worked for All Seasons almost since it's beginning in 1972. Sherry is a talented painter herself. I still enjoy a delightful picture that Sherry painted as a wedding gift for me.

All Seasons' Chicken Salad

6	cups chicken breasts, cooked and diced
1½	cups diced celery
4	tablespoons lemon juice
2	tablespoons minced onion
1	teaspoon salt
⅔	cup mayonnaise
1	package chicken flavored Ramen noodles, uncooked
2	cups seedless green grapes
1	(11-ounce) can Mandarin oranges, drained
1	(4-ounce) package, slivered almonds

Stir together chicken, celery, lemon juice, onion, and salt, Chill. Combine mayonnaise and flavor packet from Ramen noodles. Add to chicken mixture. Next add grapes, oranges, and almonds. Just before serving crumble Ramen noodles and stir in.

Mexican Chicken Salad

8	grilled chicken breasts
¾	cup mayonnaise
¾	cup sour cream
¾	cup chopped green onions
1	teaspoon cumin
1	teaspoon chili powder
1	cup chopped red bell pepper

salt and pepper to taste

| 1 | avocado, diced |

Cut the grilled chicken into bite-size pieces. Set aside. In a large bowl, combine mayonnaise, sour cream, green onions, cumin, chili powder, and bell pepper. Stir until blended; add chicken and stir to coat. Season with salt and pepper. Stir in diced avocado right before serving. Serve on a lettuce leaf or spoon into empty avocado halves.

Note: For a spicier salad add diced jalapeño!

Serving Suggestion: This salad can also be served in a pita pocket for a great sandwich. If you are making these for a tailgate party or a picnic, take the salad in a separate container and put the sandwiches together right before serving. Take along fresh tomatoes and lettuce for each sandwich. Pack a container of Stacey's salsa on page 11, along with some chips. Add some of our delicious cookies like the Hidden Kisses on page 173 and the Coconut Bars on page 187 for a delightful meal!

A unique change from your everyday chicken salad! In Texas, we like everything with a little spice. The salad can be served on a lettuce leaf or in an avocado shell. Add diced fresh garden tomatoes on top for extra color and flavor. It is also best when made with seasoned grilled chicken. Sprinkle dry fajita seasoning on your chicken before grilling for a great flavor.

Salads

A delightful salad with a unique flavor. The Chinese cabbage is milder than regular cabbage and the leaves are thin and crisp. When looking for Chinese cabbage at your local supermarket, look for crinkly, thickly veined leaves that are cream-colored with green tips.

He who refreshes others will himself be refreshed.

Proverbs 11:25

Chinese Cabbage Salad

1	medium head Chinese cabbage (Napa), chopped
2	bunches green onions, chopped
½	cup sesame seeds
1	package sliced almonds
2	packages oriental noodles, crushed
2	tablespoons margarine

Combine chopped cabbage and onions; chill in refrigerator. Saute sesame seeds, almonds, and noodles in margarine until toasted. Cool completely and add to cabbage mixture. Set aside.

Dressing:

¼	cup vinegar
¾	cup oil
½	cup sugar
2	teaspoons soy sauce
¾	cup sugar

In a saucepan, combine ingredients for dressing. Bring to a boil and boil for 1 minute. Cool completely. Right before serving, toss salad with dressing.

Green Apple Salad

1	bunch red leaf lettuce
2	Granny Smith apples
½	cup cashews, toasted
½	cup coarsely grated mild Swiss cheese

The day before serving wash lettuce and place in salad spinner or crisper. The day your serving, tear lettuce into bite-size pieces. Coarsely dice apples into ¾-inch pieces. Add cashews and cheese. Just before serving toss with Poppy Seed Dressing.

Poppy Seed Dressing

1½	cups sugar
2	teaspoons dry mustard
2	teaspoons salt
⅔	cup vinegar
2	cups cottonseed oil or vegetable oil
3	tablespoons poppy seeds

Using an electric mixer or blender, mix sugar, mustard, salt, and vinegar. Slowly add the cottonseed oil, a small amount at a time, beating constantly until thick. Add the poppy seeds and beat a few more seconds. Chill in refrigerator.

Yields: 3½ cups

Billie Jeane Garner shared this delightful apple salad. It is a nice change from the classic Waldorf. The recipe actually came from Kim Blakey who attends church with Billie at Keller United Methodist. My mom also attends that church, and I had the opportunity to meet Kim recently. Kim is very active in the church and has a true heart for helping others. After my mother had emergency surgery, Kim, like many others, brought food as soon as Mom got out of the hospital. Her thoughtfulness and that of so many others was greatly appreciated by our family!

*M*y mom, Jeanette West, had this delightful salad at Kay Meixner's house one night at Keno (or as they call it No-Keno). Marsha Conahan brought this colorful salad. Mom said the dressing just makes the salad.It is really good. Mom's Keno group is made up of teachers, some retired and some still teaching. They all enjoy getting together so much that they rarely have time to actually play Keno. Hence, they renamed their monthly event, "No-Keno!"

Spring Strawberry Salad

1	package Spring greens
1	pint fresh strawberries, sliced
1	cup toasted pecans

Mix lettuce, strawberries, and toasted pecans in a large salad bowl. Just before serving toss with dressing.

Dressing:

1½	cups sugar
2	teaspoons dry mustard
2	teaspoons salt
⅔	cup wine vinegar
1	tablespoon onion powder
1	cup olive oil
3	tablespoons poppy seeds

Mix ingredients except for oil and seeds in a saucepan. Heat until sugar dissolves and mixture starts to bubble. Add the oil, and beat with wire whisk until thickened. Remove form heat and add poppy seeds. Beat with whisk a little more. Cool and store in refrigerator. Set out in advance of serving or microwave for a few seconds before shaking to mix the ingredients. When ready to serve the salad, pour on just enough dressing to moisten the salad.

Note: This dressing keeps well. Marsha said it makes a lot so use what you need and refrigerate the rest for later.

Ambrosia Salad

1	(20-ounce) can crushed pineapple with juice
1	(6-ounce) box orange jello
2	cups buttermilk
½	cup finely chopped pecans
1	cup flaked coconut
1	(8-ounce) whipped topping, thawed

Combine pineapple with juice and jello in a saucepan. Heat just until jello is dissolved. Remove from heat; stir in buttermilk, coconut, and pecans. Fold in whipped topping. Pour into a 9x13-inch glass dish and chill until set.

Yield: 12-15 servings

Serving Suggestion: Cut into squares and serve on a lettuce leaf or pour into individual jello molds.

Helpful Hint: Spray your jello molds with nonstick cooking spray before pouring in the jello. Your salad will just slip right out. Be sure to just lightly spray the molds. Too much nonstick spray will make your jello look cloudy.

Note: Check out page 147 for Ruth's wonderful Vanilla Wafer Cake.

For years, many of us have enjoyed Ambrosia on our holiday table. This version is a delicious jello salad. The recipe was shared with me by a fellow Country Peddler exhibitor and new friend, Anne Estes. Actually the recipe is from her mother, Ruth Lewis. I told Ann that I would love to have one of her mother's recipes. The next thing I knew, she brought me a whole stack of them! I was so delighted to receive them! Ann and her dear friend, Claudine Youngblood, work together creating their products. They are such close friends, I thought they were sisters!

Yes, creating a watermelon basket takes extra time, but it adds so much to your table. Especially at a brunch or shower. See the next page for our adorable watermelon baby carriage! if you do not have time to make the melon balls, simply cut the watermelon and cantaloupe into small bite-size pieces or buy a bag of mixed frozen fruit at your local supermarket.

Note: Be sure to provide cocktail toothpicks beside the watermelon basket for your guests.

Fruit Basket Salad

1	**watermelon**
1	**cantaloupe**
1	**honeydew melon**

fresh fruits (your choice)

How to Carve A Watermelon Basket

Step 1: Place selected watermelon width-wise on a flat surface. Roll it around until it settles into a stable position or simply cut a thin slice off of the bottom. Use strips of masking tape to mark off the handle and the edge of the basket.

Step 2: Using a sharp knife, carefully cut the outside edge of the masking tape creating the handle of the basket. Next draw a decorative design around what will be the edge of the basket. You can either make a zig-zag design or use a circle template to create a scallop design.

Step 3: Cut into the melon along your design. Next, cut a large wedge from either side of the handle, leaving about an inch above your edge design. Remove the wedge. Complete your edge design. Remove any remaining fruit in the melon by cutting and scooping it out to create the inside of the basket.

Step 4: Remove the masking tape. Add a mixture of fresh fruit including the watermelon that has been cut into 1-inch cubes or made into melon balls.

Watermelon Baby Carriage

Step 1: To create the carriage canopy, use masking tape to mark off about one third, to one fourth of the watermelon, at one end. Mark off the body of the carriage by placing masking tape horizontally around the middle of the melon. Draw a zig-zag or scallop design on the tape to create a fancy edge.

Step 2: Carefully cut along the line design. Remove the rind from the top area. (It works best if you use one of the little carving saws that are sold at kitchen stores.) Set rind aside to use later for the handle. Remove tape.

Step 3: Carefully cut and scoop out the inside of the watermelon. Set aside to use later.

Step 4: To make the handle, cut out a "U" shape from the rind that was removed in step 2. Attach the handle to the carriage body with toothpicks. Use orange slices to create wheels for your carriage. Attach the wheels with wooden toothpicks or skewers. Add a melon ball or Maraschino cherry to the end of the toothpick that sticks out to complete the wheels. Note: If your carriage will not sit straight, cut a thin slice off the bottom, being careful not to cut through the rind.

Step 5: Fill with assorted melon and fresh fruit.

My sister, Karen, made this adorable watermelon baby carriage for her sister-in-law, Tamyra's baby shower. It received rave reviews!

Karen also served her favorite Old-fashion Sugar Cookies (page 174). (She tinted the icing blue since they knew it was going to be a boy). To drink she served the punch on page 28 because it is such a pretty yellow color. The table was decorated with the darling blue and yellow fabric Tamyra planned to use in the baby's nursery.

Salads

Eva Dean Stephens shared this delicious salad with us. She said it is a pretty red salad to serve at your family Christmas dinner or a holiday luncheon.

Spicy Applesauce Salad

⅔	cup red hots
2	cups boiling water
1	(6-ounce) package cherry jello
1	can applesauce

Dissolve red hots in boiling water. Remove from heat and add jello. Stir until jello has dissolved then add applesauce. Pour in a 9x13-inch pan. Chill. Serve in squares on a lettuce leaf.

Mary Wells shared this family favorite. She also said that her family would never forgive her if she did not make this salad at Christmas time. Her brother-in-law asks for this salad every year, and never shares with her sister!

Cranberry Salad

1	package fresh cranberries
1½	cups sugar
1	(15-ounce) can crushed pineapple, drained
2	cups miniature marshmallows
1	cup chopped pecans
1	cup whipped topping

Chop cranberries, stir in sugar, pineapple, and marshmallows. Let stand in the refrigerator overnight. Next day add pecans and whipped topping.

Blueberry Salad

2	(3-ounce) packages Raspberry jello
2	cups boiling water
1	can blueberries
1	small can crushed pineapple
1	(8-ounce) carton whipped topping, thawed

Dissolve jello in boiling water. Add juice from blueberries and pineapple. Remove ¾ cup of mixture. Set aside. Add blueberries and pineapple to remaining jello mixture. Pour into a 9-inch square dish. Congeal until firm. Place set aside mixture in refrigerator and allow to congeal to the consistency of egg whites. Whip this with the whipped topping and spread over congealed blueberry mixture. Refrigerate until ready to serve.

Yield: 9-12 servings

Note: This salad is very pretty. The base is purple and is filled with blueberries and pineapple. The creamy topping is pink. It makes an attractive and delicious addition to a luncheon or holiday dinner.

Kay Meixner, first had this salad when her daughter Kristina was born over 20 years ago. A good friend brought this delicious salad, and it has been a Meixner favorite ever since. Kay and my sister, Karen, first met as school teachers and became instant friends! Their classrooms connected and they taught together for the next ten years.Kay and her husband Moody have been dear friends of our entire family for over 16 years!

Salads

Another delicious salad from Eva Dean Stephens, of Farwell, Texas. This one is light and flavorful.

Peach Jello

1	(6-ounce) package peach jello
1	(8-ounce) can crushed pineapple (undrained)
3	teaspoons sugar
2	cups buttermilk
½	(8-ounce) carton whipped topping

Boil the jello, pineapple with juice, and sugar until jello and sugar are dissolved. Cool. Add the buttermilk and mix until smooth. Fold in whipped topping. Pour into a 9x13-inch dish. Refrigerate until set.

A friend of our family brought a large container of this wonderful salad to our home when my Dad passed away. Everyone loved the salad. Later when I was looking through cookbooks, I ran across a recipe for this very salad in a church cookbook. Beside the recipe was the name Mary West, my grandmother.

Pistachio Salad

1	(3-ounce) package instant Pistachio pudding mix
1	(15-ounce) can crushed pineapple with liquid
1	(12-ounce) carton whipped topping
1	cup chopped pecans
1	cup miniature marshmallow

Mix all ingredients together in a large bowl. Pour into a serving dish and cover. Refrigerate until ready to serve.

Note: This is a good salad to take for a church fellowship dinner. It is easy to make and keeps well.

Main Dishes

When Friends Gather for Fun

*Friends are those
rare people
who ask how
we are
and then wait
to hear the answer.*

*T*his savory chicken dish has been a standby for LuAnn Lemond of Hale Center for years! She has served it at covered dish dinners, graduation parties, ladies luncheons, family birthday dinners and for Sunday lunch. LuAnn suggests you serve it with wild rice and a congealed or green salad. Thank you to LuAnn for sharing this delicious recipe!

Breast of Chicken Magnificent

6-8	boneless, skinless chicken breasts (about 3-3½ pounds)
3	tablespoons flour (optional)
½	cup butter or margarine
2	cups fresh mushrooms, sliced
2	cans cream of chicken soup
1	large clove garlic, minced
	generous dash crushed thyme
⅛	teaspoon rosemary, crushed
⅓	cup light cream

Melt butter in large skillet. Toss chicken breast and flour in plastic bag to coat lightly, then brown in skillet. Remove chicken from skillet and brown mushrooms. Stir in soup, garlic, and seasonings. Return chicken to skillet, cover and cook over low heat 45 minutes, stirring occasionally. Blend in cream and heat slowly.

Note: This dish can also be baked in the oven. Just place ingredients in a 15½ x 19½ baking dish, cover with foil and bake in a 350° oven for 35 to 45 minutes until chicken is tender.

Pecan Chicken

1	cup flour
1	cup pecans, finely ground
¼	cup sesame seeds
1	tablespoon paprika
1½	teaspoons salt
⅛	teaspoon pepper
1	egg, beaten
1	cup buttermilk
8	chicken breasts, boneless, skinless
⅓	cup butter
¼	cup pecans, coarsely chopped

Combine first 6 ingredients. Mix together egg and buttermilk. Dip chicken breasts in egg mixture and coat well with flour mixture. Melt butter in a baking dish. Place chicken in dish, turning once to coat with butter. Sprinkle with coarsely chopped pecans. Bake in a preheated 350° oven for 30 minutes. Do not overcook.

Yield: 8 servings

Note: The pecans need to be finely chopped. You will need to use a nut chopper or you can use your food processor. When using your food processor, process with quick pulses until nuts are desired size. Do not overprocess or you will end up with nut butter!

Another delicious recipe from my cousin, Rosemary West. This one was in the All Seasons' 25th anniversary recipe booklet. Rosemary and her husband Robert, opened All Seasons Art and Crafts in 1972. It featured beads and macrame supplies, popular crafts at that time, and Rosemary's tole painting classes. I began working there in high school. It was my first summer job besides babysitting. I also enjoyed taking painting lessons from Rosemary. So did many others because her classes grew! She now has her own patterns and books!

*T*his delightful entree is rich and delicious. Llywlyn Walker has served it for years and says it is perfect for a graduation or bridesmaids luncheons. It is also a wonderful entree to serve when having your friends over for lunch. Instead of using one centerpiece on your luncheon table, make individual arrangements in assorted teacups or small flowerpots. This way each guest has a reminder of the luncheon. Pick up mix and match teacups on sale. Place green oasis in each cup, add water and fill with small fresh flowers. Be sure to place the cup on a saucer!

Chicken a la King

4-6	chicken breast, cooked and cut into bite size pieces
2	teaspoons salt
⅛	teaspoon pepper
⅓	cup butter or margarine
⅓	cup flour
1	cup chicken broth
1½	cups light cream
1	(2-ounce) jar pimiento strips
1	(4½-ounce) can sliced ripe olives
¼	cup slivered almonds paprika or minced parsley
6	Pepperidge Farms pastry cups

Melt butter or margarine in a medium sauce pan. Stir in flour and slowly add chicken broth and cream. Cook until thickened, stirring constantly. Add chicken, pimento, mushrooms, and ripe olives. Serve in pastry cups and top with slivered almonds, paprika, and/or parsley.

Yield: 8-10 servings

Note: Look for the pastry cups in your grocers freezer section.

Zesty Chicken Spaghetti

10-12	ounces spaghetti
1	bell pepper, chopped
1	onion, chopped
½	stick butter
3	chicken bouillon cubes
½	cup water
1	(10¾-ounce) can tomato soup
1	(10-ounce) can tomatoes and green chilies
1	(6-ounce) can sliced mushrooms (optional)
½	teaspoon salt
½	teaspoon pepper
1	teaspoon garlic powder
4	boneless skinless chicken breast, cooked and chopped into bite-size pieces
8-10	ounces Velveeta cheese, cubed
1	cup Cheddar/Jack cheese

Cook spaghetti according to package directions; drain well. In a saucepan, sauté bell pepper and onion in butter. Add water and dissolve bouillon cubes over medium heat. To the spaghetti, add bouillon mixture, soup, tomatoes, mushrooms, and seasonings. Stir to blend. Stir in chicken and Velveeta cheese. Place in two 9x13-inch glass baking dishes. Cover with foil and bake at 325° for 40 minutes. Take off foil and sprinkle on the Cheddar/Jack cheese. Return to oven for 5 minutes or until cheese melts.

A neighborhood family brought this to my mother's house to comfort us during a difficult time. My sister and I loved the spicy flavor the tomatoes and green chilies added. It was a nice change from regular chicken spaghetti.

This casserole is mild enough that most family members will enjoy it. To add a spicier kick, you could add diced jalapeños!

My daughter, Kaitlyn, loves this casserole. A family friend brought this to my mom's after a funeral. It was so good! I actually found this version in an old church cookbook from Riverside Methodist Church in Fort Worth, and the name on it was Mary West, my grandmother!

Poppy Seed Chicken and Rice Casserole

1⅓	cups uncooked rice
1	(14-ounce) can chicken broth
4	chicken breasts, cooked and diced
1	(8-ounce) carton sour cream
1	(10¾-ounce) can cream of chicken soup
1	(10¾-ounce) can cream of mushroom soup
1	tablespoon poppy seed
40	Ritz crackers, crushed
1	stick margarine, melted

Place rice in a greased 9x13-inch baking dish. Pour broth over rice. Place chicken breasts on top of rice. Combine next 5 ingredients and pour over chicken. Sprinkle crushed crackers on top. Drizzle with melted margarine. Bake in a 350° oven for 30 minutes or until bubbly.

Edith's "No-Keno" Chicken Casserole

4	large chicken breasts (with bone and skin)
2	tablespoons butter
1	green pepper, chopped
1	large onion, chopped
2	(10-ounce) cans tomatoes and green chilies
1	(10¾-ounce) can cream of mushroom soup
1	(10¾-ounce) can cream of chicken soup
12	corn tortillas, quartered
2	cups shredded Cheddar cheese

Cook chicken breasts in salted water until tender. Remove skin and bone, then shred into bite-size pieces. Reserve broth. Before assembling casserole, soak tortillas in hot broth until softened. Sauté green pepper and onion in butter. In a large bowl, combine chicken, tomatoes, soups, and sautéd vegetables. Stir until well blended. Place ½ of tortillas in bottom of a greased 9x13-inch baking dish. Top with ⅓ of chicken mixture and sprinkle with ⅔ cup of cheese. Repeat layers twice. Bake at 325° for 30 to 40 minutes. Sprinkle with remaining cheese and bake 5 additional minutes. Let set for 15 minutes before serving.

Note: Edith suggests cooking chicken breasts with the skin and bone on them because it adds more flavor to the meat. I would have to agree!

Edith Shallene has the gift of hospitality! She has been a dear friend of our family for many years. She and my mother taught 2nd grade together for over 15 years. Recently when I was visiting Mom it was the monthly Keno night and it was at Edith's. She served this delicious casserole. Now, I have had a lot of King Ranch casseroles, but this one was the best! Their Keno night is filled with more talking and eating than playing the game, hence their name "No-Keno Night"!

*M*y kids love this casserole! Probably because of the chips and cheese on top. Either way it is a nice change of pace from the usual chicken strip dinner!

Note: Be sure to put the cheese on, then the chips. This way the chips stay crunchy.

Be kind and compassionate to one another, forgiving each other, just as in Christ God forgave you.
Eph. 4:32

Crunchy Chicken Salad Casserole

3	boneless-skinless chicken breasts, cooked and cubed
¾	cup diced celery
1	tablespoon onion, finely chopped
¾	cup sliced almonds
1½	cups cooked rice
1	(10¾-ounce) can cream of chicken soup
1	tablespoon lemon juice
½	teaspoon salt
¼	teaspoon pepper
¾	cup mayonnaise
¼	cup chicken broth
1½	cups shredded Cheddar cheese
1½	cups crushed potato chips

Combine first 9 ingredients. Mix well and set aside. Combine mayonnaise and broth; whisk until smooth. Add to chicken mixture and stir well. Spoon into a greased 9x13-inch baking dish. Bake at 400° for 15 to 20 minutes. Add cheese then sprinkle chips on top. Return to oven for 5 more minutes or until cheese melts. Serve hot.

Yield: 8-10 servings

Grilled Chicken with Corn and Roasted Pepper Relish

6	boneless, skinless chicken breasts
6	tablespoons olive oil
3	teaspoons ground cumin
2	teaspoons ground thyme
1	teaspoon fresh ground pepper
½	teaspoon cayenne
½	teaspoon salt

Combine olive oil, spices, and salt. Lay chicken breasts in a shallow pan and cover with ¾ of oil mixture. Allow chicken to marinade in refrigerator for at least two hours. Place chicken breasts on grill. Use reserved marinade to baste each chicken breast liberally before and after turning. Cover and cook for 4 minutes on each side or until juices run clear.

Relish:

2	cups fresh corn kernels
1	cup chopped roasted bell peppers
⅔	cup chopped tomato
½	cup chopped green onions
2	tablespoons chopped fresh cilantro
2	teaspoons minced, seeded jalapeño peppers
2	tablespoons fresh lime juice

salt and pepper to taste

Combine all ingredients and serve over chicken.

Add color and pizazz to grilled chicken with this delicious relish! Follow the instructions below for roasting peppers. Use a combination of peppers for a colorful relish. Combine the ingredients several hours ahead of time or refrigerate overnight so the flavors have time to blend together.
To roast bell peppers: Cut in half, seed, then place on a baking sheet, skin side up. Place 3 to 4 inches from broiler and char until the skins are blackened. Put them in a plastic or paper bag, seal, and let stand 15 minutes. Remove from bag and peel off the skin. Chop for relish.

109

*M*y husband, Dell, makes the BEST chicken fajitas. He would not let me put them in the first cookbook because he said they were too simple. But so many people that have enjoyed these at our home asked for his recipe and helpful hints. He finally agreed to write it down. This is one of our favorite summer meals. We serve it so often to friends that our kids started calling it THE Fajita Dinner. Our kids may grow tired of it, but our guests have not. Our friends continue to pass their plates for more!

Dell's Grilled Chicken Fajitas

1	bottle Claude's fajita marinade, divided
6	large boneless, skinless chicken breasts
½	cup cooking oil

Place chicken in a large glass baking dish. Pour ¾ bottle of Claude's marinade over chicken; cover and refrigerate over night. Before grilling, pour cooking oil over chicken and make sure each piece is well oiled before placing on grill. Preheat grill and get it very hot. Place chicken on grill to sear then lower heat to medium. Discard marinade. Cook for 5 to 7 minutes then turn and cook for an additional 3 to 5 minutes. Baste frequently with basting sauce (see recipe below). Chicken is done when it feels firm to the touch and juices run clear when pierced. DO NOT overcook! Slice into strips and serve with warm flour tortillas and grilled peppers and onions. (See next page.)

Basting Sauce:

½	stick butter
¼	bottle Claude's fajita marinade

Melt butter then add marinade. Mix well. Baste chicken frequently while it cooks.

Yield: serves 6-8 people

Grilled Peppers and Onions

3	large bell peppers (use one each; yellow, red and green)
1-2	large onions
1	teaspoon California-style garlic powder
1	teaspoon salt
2	tablespoons olive oil

Slice peppers into strips and onions into rings. Place oil in a large skillet then add peppers and onions. Sprinkle with garlic powder and salt. Saute until crisp tender. Do not cook too long or they will be mushy.

Yield: serves 6-8 people

This is the way Dell prepares the peppers and onions for fajitas. The addition of the garlic powder gives them a wonderful flavor. Warm a platter and place the peppers, onions, and grilled chicken on it to serve.

Pico de Gallo

¾	cup chopped fresh tomatoes
½	cup onion, diced
½	cup green bell pepper, diced
½	fresh jalapeño, seeded and minced
1	tablespoon fresh cilantro, chopped
½	teaspoon California-style garlic powder
	salt to taste

Combine ingredients then refrigerate for 30 minutes to 1 hour before serving.

Not only tasty, but also colorful. Pico de Gallo is always served with Dell's Fajitas. Remember to make it ahead of time so the flavors will have a chance to blend.

*D*elicious!
A unique combination
of flavors. The
caramelized onions
combine with the
barbeque sauce to
create an incredible
pizza!

Barbeque Chicken Pizza

bread machine pizza dough
your favorite barbeque sauce
2   cups grilled or roasted
         chicken, shredded
caramelized onions (optional)
2   cups mozzarella cheese

Make pizza dough (see recipe on next page) and press out to cover a 16-inch pizza pan. Cover dough with a thin layer of barbeque sauce. Top with chicken, caramelized onions, and cheese. Bake in a 450° oven for 15 to 20 minutes or until the crust is browned and the cheese is bubbly.

Note: Cook on the bottom rack of your oven so the bottom of the pizza gets nice and brown.

Note: This pizza is great with grilled chicken, but if you are short on time, use precooked roasted chicken that is available at your local grocery store.

*W*hen available
use a sweet onion like
the Texas 1015 for a
wonderful flavor!

Caramelized Onions

2   teaspoons olive oil
2   medium onions, thinly sliced
2   teaspoons sugar

Place olive oil in a large, nonstick skillet and heat. Cook onion and sugar in hot oil over low heat stirring often. Cook for 20 to 25 minutes or until onion is tender and a caramel color.

Bread Machine Pizza Dough

3	cups all-purpose flour
1	teaspoon salt
2	teaspoons active dry yeast
1	tablespoon sugar
2	tablespoons olive oil
1	cup warm water

Note: for Welbilt and Dak machines, add 2 additional tablespoons of water.

Place all ingredients in the bread machine, select the "dough" setting and start the machine. If time allows, let the machine complete the full kneading and rising cycle. In a hurry? (I usually am) Stop the machine after the first kneading cycle. Transfer the dough to a pizza pan that has been sprayed with nonstick cooking spray. Shape dough to fit pan leaving a rim around the edge to hold ingredients in. Spread desired sauce then add toppings and cheese. Bake on the bottom rack of a 450° oven for 15 to 20 minutes or until crust is golden brown and cheese is bubbly.

Note: If you like garlic as much as we do, you can use garlic infused olive oil in the crust for a wonderful flavor!

Easy to make, this recipe makes the best pizza crust! It uses basic ingredients and takes no time at all.

For fun let you kids make their own individual pizzas.

Note: If you do not have a pizza pan simply shape it on a large cookie sheet or on a baking stone if you have one.

113

*D*ell created this incredibly delicious entree. We both like peppered steaks so he tried a pepper rub on roast beef. The result was outstanding! It is spicy and goes well with mashed potatoes (recipe page 70). The drippings also make a beautiful mahogany colored gravy that has a spicy kick to it.

Roast Gravy

1¾   cups roast drippings
2   tablespoons cornstarch
salt to taste

Spoon grease from drippings. If there are not enough drippings, add water and stir to dissolve baked on juices. Pour liquid into a small sauce pan. Dissolve corn starch in ¼ cup cold water. Stir cornstarch into drippings. Season to taste. Bring to a boil, stirring constantly. Boil for 1 minute or until gravy thickens.

114

Pepper Crusted Roast Beef

1	(9 - 12 pound) rump roast
1	cup coarsely ground black pepper
1	teaspoon California-style garlic
1	teaspoon paprika
1	teaspoon dried oregano
1	tablespoon granulated beef stock base
1	teaspoon cornstarch
olive oil	

Mix all dry ingredients together. Liberally coat roast with olive oil. (pour on, then brush to completely cover roast top side and bottom) Encrust roast by pouring small amounts of the pepper mixture on the roast and patting down with the back side of a wooden spoon to make it stick. Do this until the entire roast is completely covered with pepper, top and bottom. Place meat in a roasting pan with a rack. Insert a meat thermometer into the center part of the roast. Cook in a 325° oven for approximately 30 minutes per pound or until the thermometer reaches 160° or medium. Let the meat rest for at least 15 minutes before cutting.

Note: It is best to remove the roast a little before it reaches 160° because it will continue to cook for a few minutes after it is removed. It is also good to let a piece of meat rest after cooking so the juices will not run out when sliced.

Southwest Roast

1	(3-5 pound) trimmed brisket
1½	cups pinto beans
1	teaspoon salt
½	teaspoon pepper
1	teaspoon garlic powder
1	(10-ounce) can tomatoes and green chilies
1	(7-ounce) can chopped green chilies
2	(10¾-ounce) cans cream of mushroom soup

Cover beans with water and soak over night. Drain beans and place in the bottom of a large roasting pan. Sprinkle with salt, pepper and garlic powder. Cover with water and set meat on top of beans. Top with remaining ingredients and bake covered in a 225° oven for 15 to 18 hours.

To serve: Shred roast and serve with flour tortillas, grated cheese, sour cream, and salsa.

Note: We add additional salt to ours when cooking. Cathy also said if you are cooking it the full 18 hours you do not have to soak the beans the night before.

This entree is easy to prepare, feeds a lot of people, and is wonderful! It is the perfect recipe for busy moms. I love that you just put it on and let it cook. It is the perfect thing to serve when you have a house full of company coming and no time to cook! Cathy Davis, who has cut my hair for years, shared this wonderful recipe. Cathy is one of the hardest working and most dedicated people I have ever met. She is always smiling and willing to listen. She and I have shared the joys and tears of raising kids and will continue to do so for many years to come!

Main Dishes

A nice change of pace, this quiche is easy to make and delicious! It is hearty enough to please the men in your family. Even my teenagers enjoy it. Serve with a pretty green salad like Martha's Garden Fresh Salad on page 82 or the Mandarin Orange Salad on page 86.

Friendship consists in forgetting what one gives, and remembering what one receives.

Green Chile Beef Quiche

1	unbaked 9-inch, deep dish pie shell
2½	cups ground beef
¼	cup onion
2	teaspoons chili powder, divided
½	teaspoon California-style garlic powder
1	teaspoon salt
1	(7-ounce) can diced green chilies
2	cups Cheddar cheese
1½	cups evaporated milk
½	cup milk
4	eggs
1	teaspoon cumin
½	teaspoon seasoned salt

Preheat oven to 375°. In a skillet, cook ground beef and onion until meat is no longer pink. Drain well. Stir in 1 teaspoon chili powder, garlic powder, and salt. Place pie shell on a cookie sheet. (This makes it easier to handle and also helps keep your oven clean.) Spoon meat into pie shell. Sprinkle green chilies and cheese over meat. Combine evaporated milk, regular milk, eggs, comino, 1 teaspoon chili powder, and seasoned salt. Whisk until well blended. Carefully pour egg mixture over meat and cheese. Bake for 40 to 45 minutes. Remove from oven and let sit for at least 10 minutes before serving.

Taco Bake

1	pound ground beef
1	small onion, chopped
¾	cup water
1	package dry taco seasoning
1	(15-ounce) can tomato sauce
1	(4-ounce) can chopped green chilies
salt and pepper to taste	
1	(12-ounce) package shell macaroni
¾	cup sour cream
2	cups Cheddar/Jack cheese, grated

In a skillet, brown ground beef and onion. Drain well. Add water, taco seasoning, tomato sauce, and green chilies. Bring to a boil; reduce heat and simmer 20 minutes. While meat mixture is simmering prepare shell macaroni. Cook according to package directions. Drain macaroni and stir into meat mixture. Add sour cream; stir until ingredients are blended. Grease a 9 x 13-inch baking dish with nonstick cooking spray. Pour in noodle/beef mixture. Bake for 15 minutes then add cheese and bake until cheese is melted and casserole is bubbly.

Yield: Serves 8-10

Filled with the wonderful flavors of tacos, this easy to make casserole is sure to please your family, or a house full of teenagers!

We fall down by ourselves, but it takes a friendly hand to lift us up.

This has to be the most unique and original recipe I received. Ginny Secor sent us this incredible casserole. Ginny was my sister's roommate in college. She is now married and lives in Georgia. She is also the mother of two adorable boys! Ginny often prepares this casserole for friends who have just had a baby because it freezes so well. It is a great change of pace. Serve it when your are looking for something out of the ordinary.

Black Bean and Rice Layered Casserole

1	(8-ounce) package of black bean and rice mix (e.g., Mahatma, Vigo, etc.)
4	(6-ounce) packages cream cheese, softened
4	flour tortillas
1	(14-ounce) can diced tomatoes, do not drain
1	large onion, chopped
4	tablespoons cilantro, chopped
1	(1-pound) roll breakfast sausage, cooked and drained
4	cups Cheddar cheese, grated

Preheat oven to 350°. Prepare bean and rice mix according to package directions. Fold in cream cheese. In a 9x13-inch greased casserole dish, layer the following: 2 tortillas, ½ of bean and rice mixture, ½ of sausage, ½ of tomatoes with liquid and ½ of onions. Sprinkle with 2 tablespoons of cilantro and 2 cups Cheddar cheese. Repeat layers starting with the tortillas. Bake for 20 minutes. Edges and cheese should be bubbly. Cut into squares and serve with sour cream.

Yield: 6 to 8 servings

Roast Pork with Sour Cream Gravy

4-5	cloves garlic
1½	teaspoons salt, divided
1	(3 to 3½-pound) boneless double pork loin roast, tied
2	tablespoons lemon juice
¼	cup butter, melted
½	teaspoon freshly ground pepper

Preheat oven to 325°. Cut garlic cloves in thin slices. Sprinkle garlic with ¼ teaspoon salt. Cut two rows of ½-inch slits in top of roast at 1-inch intervals. Insert garlic slices deep into the slits. Combine butter and lemon juice. Brush roast with butter mixture, sprinkle with pepper and 1¼ teaspoon of remaining salt. Insert meat thermometer. Bake, uncovered, for 30 minutes per pound or until thermometer reads 160°. When done, let stand for 15 minutes before slicing. Serve with Sour Cream Gravy.

An elegant and delicious entree!

Sour Cream Gravy

1½	cups sliced fresh mushrooms
2	tablespoons butter, melted
1	tablespoon all-purpose flour
1	(8-ounce) carton sour cream
2	tablespoons milk
¼	teaspoon salt
¼	teaspoon freshly ground pepper

In a small saucepan, Cook mushrooms in butter over medium high heat until tender. Add flour and cook for 1 minute, stirring constantly. Remove from heat. Combine sour cream with milk, salt, and pepper. Gradually add sour cream mixture to mushroom mixture, stirring constantly. Cook over medium-low heat, stirring constantly, until mixture thickens. Do not allow to boil.

119

A great crockpot recipe! This one comes from Daisy Langford, my good friend Liz Langford's, mother-in-law. It is similar to a recipe my sister served at her son Clay's graduation. It is delicious and feeds a crowd! Cooking it in the crockpot makes the pork extremely tender and moist. It is a great recipe because it cooks while your are busy doing other things!

Note: If your kids do not like beans you can leave them out. My sister, Karen, cooks beans in a separate crockpot, that way everybody is happy.

Upside-Down Chalupa

1	pound dried pinto beans (soaked in water overnight)
1	(2½-pound) pork loin roast
¼	teaspoon garlic powder
1	teaspoon cumin seed
1	teaspoon oregano
1	teaspoon Tabasco sauce
1	teaspoon salt
1	(10-ounce) can tomatoes and chilies
1	(7½-ounce) can jalapeño relish
1	cup water
2	tablespoons chili powder

Place all ingredients in a crockpot and cook on low heat overnight. Serve over chips and top with grated Cheddar cheese.

Serving Suggestion: We like to serve ours with warm flour tortillas, cheese, sour cream, and salsa! We roll it up like a fajita.

The ornaments of our house are the friends that frequent it.

Ralph Waldo Emerson

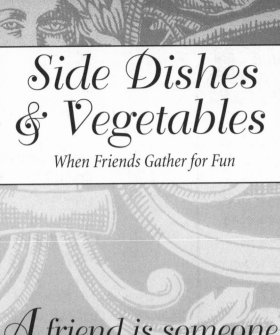

Side Dishes & Vegetables

When Friends Gather for Fun

A friend is someone who understands your past, believes in your future, and accepts you today just the way you are.

*C*athleen Turner, a painting student of my cousin Rosemary West, shared this delicious recipe. Rosemary enjoyed it so much that she passed it on to me. It is a nice change and a pretty way to serve carrots.

*S*ue White, our good friend, passed along this yummy corn recipe. Her daughter-in-law, Kimbra Carson of Plainview, prepares this casserole often for family gatherings. It tastes great and is easy enough to make for any family meal.

Carrot Souffle

2	pounds carrots, cooked and drained
½	cup sugar
1	stick margarine
1	tablespoon vanilla
3	eggs

Peel carrots, cut into pieces and boil until tender. Drain well. Combine cooked carrots and remaining ingredients in food processor. Blend together until smooth. Pour into greased baking dish. Bake at 350° for 45 minutes or until center is set.

Corn Casserole

1	(14.75-ounce) can whole kernel corn, drained
1	(15-ounce) can cream style corn
2	eggs
3	tablespoons flour
¼	cup sugar
½	cup margarine, melted
1	roll Ritz Crackers

Mix first 5 ingredients together in a mixing bowl. Melt ½ cup margarine in a 9x13-inch baking dish. Pour corn mixture in dish and bake in a 325° oven for 30 minutes. Remove from oven and cover with crushed Ritz crackers (approximately 1 roll). Return to oven and bake 20-30 minutes more.

Mrs. Adams
Corn Casserole

6	green onions, chopped
1	green bell pepper, chopped
1	stick margarine,
1	(14½-ounce) can cream style corn
1	(12-ounce) can whole corn, drained
1	egg
1	(6-ounce) package yellow cornbread mix
1	cup shredded cheese (any kind)
1	(2-ounce) jar diced pimento

Cook onion, bell pepper, and margarine in microwave for 3 minutes. Combine all other ingredients mixing by hand; do not use an electric mixer. Bake in a greased 2-quart casserole dish at 350° for 45 minutes.

Note: I use Cheddar cheese.

Mrs. Adam's said her family always looks forward to this casserole at Thanksgiving. It would also be a great dish to take to the church potluck or to comfort a friend.

*O*ne of the most enjoyable parts of promoting my first cookbook is all of the new friends I have made! Bobbie Adams is one of the most delightful store owners I have ever met! She cooked for weeks preparing for my book signing. When I arrived, she had prepared the most beautiful table filled with goodies out of our first cookbook, "Where Hearts Gather". Bobbie greeted each customer warmly and by name. It is no wonder that Adam's Gift Shop in Round Rock, Texas, has been successful for many years. She is retired now, but new owners carry on her legacy.

123

*P*aula Johnson
always brings the
baked beans for our
annual 4th of July Party.
The recipe is from
her Grandmother
McClellan. Paula said it
is like a lot of recipes
passed on because her
grandmother never
measured. She just
made them! Paula
wrote the recipe down
for me and said this
was as close as she
could get! I made them,
and they taste just like
the ones she brings on
the 4th. The fried bacon
and the bacon drippings
give the beans a
wonderful flavor!

Paula's Baked Beans

1	(31-ounce) can Van Camp's pork and beans
1	(15-ounce) can Van Camp's pork and beans
3-4	slices of bacon (good quality, thick-sliced)
1	large onion, chopped
⅓	cup ketchup
¾	cup brown sugar
1	tablespoon prepared mustard
1	tablespoon Worcestershire sauce

Preheat oven to 400°. Fry bacon until crisp. Cool and coarsely crumble. Cook onions in bacon drippings until tender. In a deep baking dish that has been generously sprayed with nonstick cooking spray, combine all ingredients including all of bacon drippings. Bake at 400° for approximately 1 hour until no longer soupy.

Note: Sometimes canned pork and beans can contain more liquid than necessary. Drain some of the excess liquid off before using. When all ingredients are combined the mixture should be thick.

Helpful Hint from Paula: If in a hurry, once assembled beans can be microwaved until hot and then baked 30 to 40 minutes in your conventional oven.

French Bean Casserole

2	(14½-ounce) cans French-style green beans
1	(10¾-ounce) can cream of mushroom soup
1½	cups Cheddar cheese, grated
¼	cup milk
fresh ground pepper to taste	
1	(6-ounce) can mushrooms
1	(8-ounce) can water chestnuts drained and cut into quarters
1	(2.8-ounce) can French-fried onion rings

Heat beans then drain well. While hot, add mushroom soup, cheese, milk, and pepper. Stir in mushrooms and water chestnuts. Place in a shallow baking dish; cover with onion rings. Bake at 350° for approximately 15 minutes or until bubbly and onions are brown and crisp.

Yield: 6-8 servings

Serving Suggestion: Try this recipe with regular canned green beans instead of the French-style.

A nice change from your everyday green bean casserole. The creamy cheese sauce is delicious and the water chestnuts give it an extra crunch!

Note: I prefer to cook the casserole without the onion rings for the 15 minutes. I then add the onion rings on top and cook for 5 more minutes. This keeps the onion rings from getting too brown.

*M*artha Birdwell shares this sinfully delicious recipe. She said her children gave this recipe its name. Every time she would serve them, they would say, "These are so good, they are just down right sinful!" So the name "Sin Spuds" evolved. Martha says she never has any of these leftover. It seems no matter how much she makes, it is never enough!

Sin Spuds

10-12	red new potatoes, washed and scrubbed
1	stick butter
1	(16-ounce) carton sour cream
½-¾	cup milk
salt, pepper, and garlic powder to taste	
6	green onions, chopped
10	strips bacon, fried and crumbled
1½	cups grated Cheddar cheese

Boil potatoes until tender. Mash with skins on. Stir in butter, sour cream, and enough milk to make creamy. Add salt, pepper, and garlic powder to taste. Pour into a casserole dish. Sprinkle top with chopped green onions, bacon, and cheese. Bake in a 350° oven for 25 minutes.

Fiesta Potatoes

2	pounds red potatoes, washed and cut into chunks
1	teaspoon salt
2	ounces cream cheese
½	stick butter
½	cup warm milk
1	cup shredded Cheddar/Jack cheese mix
¼	teaspoon California-style garlic powder
¼	cup diced pimento, drained
⅓	cup diced green onion
	dash of cayenne pepper
	salt and pepper to taste

Wash potatoes thoroughly. Remove eyes and any bad spots but do not peel. Cut into chunks and place in a large pan, add 1 teaspoon salt and just cover with water. Cook uncovered on medium-high until tender. Drain and add cream cheese and butter. Mash with potato masher or whip with mixer, gradually adding warm milk. Stir in cheese and remaining ingredients. Mix until well blended.

Yield: 4-6 servings

A Tex-Mex version of mashed potatoes with just the right blend of flavors. This new recipe is one that I created from a combination of recipes. It is quickly becoming one of our family's favorites! It is delicious with chicken or steak.

Happy is the house that shelters a friend.

*M*y daughter, Kaitlyn, loves potatoes prepared just about any way you can make them. She loves the Hash Brown Casserole in our first cookbook. This one is just a little different from that one. It uses Parmesan cheese and adds the pimento and green pepper for a colorful dish. If you liked the first recipe try this one. I am sure you will like it too!

Party Potato Casserole

2	(10¾-ounce) cans cream of celery soup
1	(8-ounce) carton sour cream
1	medium onion, chopped
1	green pepper, chopped
3	tablespoons diced pimento
2	teaspoons salt
⅛	teaspoon pepper
1	(32-ounce) bag frozen hash brown potatoes
¼	cup grated Parmesan cheese (optional)
⅛	teaspoon paprika (optional)

In a large mixing bowl, combine first 7 ingredients and mix well. Stir in potatoes. Spread potato mixture in an ungreased 9x13-inch baking dish or a 3-quart casserole. Sprinkle with Parmesan cheese; cover and bake in a 325° oven for 60 minutes. Remove cover and bake for an additional 30 minutes or until potatoes are tender. Sprinkle with paprika if desired.

Note: Do not thaw the hash browns. If you do, it will make your casserole mushy.

Sue's Layered Potato Casserole

8-10	potatoes, peeled and cooked
1	teaspoon salt
½	pound Velveeta cheese, grated
½	pound Cheddar cheese, grated
½	cup chopped onion
salt and pepper to taste	
1	cup salad dressing
½	pound bacon, cooked crisp
1	(4¼-ounce) can chopped black olives
1	(6-ounce) box garlic croutons

Peel and boil potatoes in salted water until tender. Dice cooked potatoes. In a large mixing bowl, combine potatoes, both cheeses, and onions. Salt and pepper to taste. Spray a 9x13-inch baking dish with nonstick cooking spray. Spread potato mixture in baking dish and layer salad dressing on top of potatoes. (use enough to cover potato mixture) Cover and refrigerate for several hours or overnight. Crumble crisp bacon on top of potatoes then sprinkle with olives. Cover with croutons and bake in a 350° oven for 1 hour.

Yield:8-10 servings

Note: For variation, use sliced green olives instead of black olives.

A delicious recipe from our good friend Sue White. This one is unique because you layer the ingredients and then refrigerate it for awhile before you cook it. This is a great make ahead dish. Prepare it the night before company comes. The next day cook the bacon and put the casserole in the oven an hour before your guests arrive.

Donna Parker teaches with my sister Karen in Edmond, Oklahoma. Donna is a great cook and this recipe for potato seasonings is one of her family's favorites. It makes a lot of the seasoning so you can have it on hand.

There is no possession more valuable than a good and faithful friend.

Parker Potatoes

Seasoning:

½	cup beef bullion granules
1½	tablespoons fine pepper
1½	tablespoons coarse pepper
2	tablespoons onion powder
2	tablespoons garlic powder
1	tablespoon paprika
1½	tablespoons salt
¼	cup flour
½	cup Parmesan cheese

Combine all ingredients; stir to blend seasonings. Place in an empty spice jar.

To make potatoes:

Quarter potatoes lengthwise into wedges; leave skins on. Oil lightly. (I dip the wedges in melted butter). Sprinkle with seasoning mixture. Bake at 350° for 45 minutes to 1 hour. Serve with Ranch dressing!

Note: To serve as an appetizer, sprinkle with cheese and bacon crumbles when you take them out of the oven. Serve with sour cream or ranch dressing.

Squash Olé

4-5	cups yellow squash, cooked and drained
1	teaspoon salt
½	teaspoon freshly ground pepper
1	small onion, chopped
1	(7-ounce) can chopped green chilies, drained
1½	cups grated Monterey Jack cheese
1	(10¾-ounce) can cream of chicken soup
1	cup sour cream
1	stick butter, melted
1	package herb stuffing mix

Boil squash in salted water until tender; drain well. In a large mixing bowl, combine squash, salt, pepper, onions, green chilies, cheese, soup, and sour cream. Mix well. In a separate bowl, toss stuffing mix with melted butter. Stir ½ of buttered stuffing mix into squash mixture. Pour into a 9x13-inch baking dish that has been sprayed with nonstick cooking spray. Top with remaining stuffing mixture. Bake uncovered, in a 375° oven for 30 minutes.

Yield: 10 to 12 servings

This is my favorite squash casserole. I first made this last summer when we had an abundance of squash in our summer garden. I shared the recipe with several of our customers at the Farmer's Market where we sold our produce. They liked it so much they came back for more squash! I love the flavor that the green chilies and Monterey Jack cheese add.

Note: Squash has a lot of water in it. Be sure to drain it really well after cooking and before you mix in the other ingredients. Otherwise your casserole will be too soupy.

131

*T*ry this recipe with fresh summer tomatoes. Our favorites are the large beefy Heirloom varieties. Last summer we grew several different Heirloom tomatoes. They are unique in both color and flavor. Many people say the flavor reminds them of the tomatoes their grandparents grew in their garden. If you are fortunate enough to have a farmers market near by, look for Purple Cherokee tomatoes. They are not much to look at, but the flavor is out of this world!

Tejas Tomatoes

3	medium-size tomatoes, halved
2	tablespoons Italian oil and vinegar dressing
2	tablespoons butter, melted
6	rounded teaspoons bread crumbs
2	teaspoons grated Parmesan cheese
¼	teaspoon garlic, minced

Arrange tomato halves in broiling pan. Pour 1 teaspoon Italian dressing on each. Combine melted butter, bread crumbs, cheese, and garlic; mix thoroughly. Place bread crumb mixture on each tomato half. Place under broiler and lightly brown. Serve warm.

Yield: 6 servings

Note: Add fresh herbs like basil for additional flavor, or try using seasoned bread crumbs.

Zucchini Corn Medley

3	small zucchini
1	tablespoon butter or margarine
1	tablespoon vegetable oil
1-2	garlic cloves, minced
1	(15-ounce) can whole kernel corn, drained
1	(2-ounce) jar diced pimiento, drained
1	teaspoon salt
¾	teaspoon lemon pepper
½	cup shredded mozzarella cheese
2	tablespoons fresh basil, chopped

Cut zucchini into quarters then thinly slice each quarter. In a large skillet, heat butter and vegetable oil over medium-high heat. Sauté zucchini and garlic for 3 to 4 minutes. Add corn, pimiento, salt, and lemon pepper. Cook until zucchini is tender, stirring often. (approximately 2 to 3 minutes) Sprinkle with shredded cheese and basil. Heat until cheese is melted.

Note: This recipe is wonderful with canned corn but even better with 2 cups of fresh corn kernels. (about 4 ears of corn)

Add a little color to your meal with this quick and easy recipe. It is very flavorful and especially good when prepared with fresh summer sweet corn and garden fresh zucchini. Our favorite summer corn is the sweet bi-colored corn.

Do not substitute dried basil for the fresh. If you do not have an herb garden, check with your local grocer. Many are now carrying a variety of fresh herbs.

A summer favorite that uses wonderful garden fresh vegetables and herbs. This dish is easy to make and colorful!

Summer Vegetable Casserole

3-4	medium, yellow summer squash
3	medium tomatoes, sliced
1	medium onion, thinly sliced
⅓	cup grated Parmesan cheese
1	teaspoon fresh basil
½	teaspoon thyme
1	teaspoon seasoned salt

In a 2-quart casserole, layer half of squash, onions, and tomatoes. Sprinkle with half of cheese, basil, thyme, and salt. Repeat with remaining ingredients. Cover with plastic wrap and microwave on high for 10-12 minutes or until vegetables are tender.

A ttractive and colorful, this is a nice side dish to brighten up any dinner plate! You can also add fresh chopped herbs to this for more flavor.

Squash & Carrot Julienne

¾	lb. unpeeled zucchini
¾	lb. carrots, peeled
¾	lb. unpeeled yellow squash
½	cup butter, room temperature
	salt and pepper to taste
	freshly grated Parmesan cheese

Cut zucchini, carrots, and squash in ¼-inch julienne strips. Steam julienned vegetables in a steamer over 1 inch of boiling water. When vegetables are tender-crisp, remove from steamer and toss with butter, salt, and pepper. Sprinkle with Parmesan cheese if desired.

Mother's Cornbread Dressing

1	stick margarine, melted
1	onion, chopped
chopped celery- (to personal taste)	
6-8	hard-boiled eggs, chopped
1	pan cooled cornbread, crumbled
1	teaspoon sage
1	teaspoon baking powder
Pan drippings from turkey or use chicken broth	
salt and pepper to taste	

Cook chopped onions and celery in stick of melted margarine. Mix chopped eggs, crumbled cornbread, sage, and baking powder together in a large bowl. Add cooked onions and celery. Add chicken or turkey broth. If mixture seems dry add milk or buttermilk until mixture is moist. Place in a greased baking dish and bake at 350° for 45 minutes, until top is brown and crusty.

A wonderful recipe from Sue Haney's mother, Winona Jones. This dressing is one of their family's holiday favorites. It is a good accompaniment any time to chicken or turkey. Sue said it is especially nice because the dressing is light, fluffy and does not have too much sage. She also shared that their whole family tends to fuss over who gets the crusty corner pieces. They are everyone's favorite. Later in the day they also enjoy it cold with leftover turkey and cranberry sauce.

We love any kind of Mexican food, and when we discovered this flavorful side dish, it quickly became a favorite. It is mild yet flavorful with the cilantro and the Mexican Velveeta. You could spice it up with the addition of diced jalapeños.

Cilantro is also called Chinese parsley and coriander. It can be found year-round in most supermarkets and is usually sold in bunches. It has a pungent fragrance and is dark green.

Mexican Festival Corn and Rice Casserole

2	cups uncooked converted rice
2	tablespoons butter
¾	cup chopped green bell pepper
¾	cup diced onion
1	(15½-ounce) can cream style corn
1	cup whole kernel corn
1	(10-ounce) can diced tomatoes with lime juice and cilantro
1	(8-ounce) block of mild Mexican Velveeta, cubed
¾	teaspoon salt
¼	teaspoon pepper
1	cup grated Cheddar cheese

Cook rice according to package directions. In a large skillet, melt butter; sauté peppers and onions until tender. Stir in rice, cream-style corn, whole kernel corn and next 4 ingredients. Transfer to a 9x13-inch baking dish that has been sprayed lightly with nonstick cooking spray. Bake uncovered in a 350° oven for 30 minutes or until thoroughly heated. Top with Cheddar cheese and return to oven for an additional 5 minutes or until cheese is melted.

Yield: 10-12 servings

Spanish Rice

⅓   cup vegetable oil
½   cup chopped onion
½   cup chopped green pepper
1   cup uncooked converted rice
¼   teaspoon California-style
      garlic powder
2   (11.5-ounce) cans V-8 juice
dash of cayenne pepper
salt and fresh ground pepper to taste

Sauté rice, onions, and green pepper until rice begins to turn yellow, approximately 5 minutes. Add garlic powder and V-8 juice. Stir; cover and simmer for 20 minutes. Stir in cayenne, salt, and pepper. Fluff with a fork and serve.

A repeat from our first cookbook, but this is the best Spanish rice recipe I have ever found. It is especially good with Dell's Fajitas on page 110.

Rice Con Queso

1   cup uncooked rice
2   cups chicken broth
1   pint sour cream
1   (7-ounce) can chopped green
      chilies
1   (8-ounce) package grated
      Cheddar/Jack cheese
½   cup water
1   teaspoon granulated beef
      bouillon

Cook rice in 2 cups of chicken broth. Combine cooked rice and remaining ingredients. Spoon into a lightly greased baking dish. Bake uncovered in a 350° oven for 30 minutes.

Another flavorful side dish. Serve with steak, chicken, or grilled pork chops. Sprinkle a little chopped cilantro on top for extra flavor.

*T*his is another family favorite from the Hatch family cookbook. This one comes from Leta Hatch. My dear friend and coffee buddy, Liz Langford, shared the Hatch family cookbook with me. It is from her mother-in-law's family who are all wonderful cooks. Liz and I have been friends since our kids were in preschool. And since our kids are now teenagers, that is a long time!!

Texas Rice

½   cup butter or margarine
1   cup chopped green onion
4   cups cooked rice
2   cups sour cream
1   cup cream-style cottage
        cheese
½   teaspoon salt
2   (4-ounce) cans chopped
        green chilies
2   cups grated Cheddar cheese

Melt butter in a medium skillet. Sauté peppers and onions over medium-high heat until tender. In a large bowl, combine peppers and onions with remaining ingredients; mix well. Transfer mixture to a 2-quart casserole dish and bake, uncovered, in a 375° oven for 25 minutes.

Note: For a taste of the Texas coast, add chopped boiled shrimp!

A true friend is one who hears and understands when you share your deepest feelings...
prods you to personal growth, stretches you to your full potential.
And most amazing of all, celebrates your successes as if they were her own.

Cakes & Pies

When Friends Gather for Dessert

Friendship Cake

1 cup of greetings
1 large hug
1 teaspoon sympathy
1/2 cup of smiles
2/3 cup of love
2 cups of hospitality

Cream greetings and smiles thoroughly. Add hugs. Slowly stir in love. Sift sympathy and hospitality and fold in carefully. Bake in a warm heart. Serve often.

Cakes

*O*ur family has enjoyed this cake for many years. I always thought it was one of my grandmother's recipes. As I was working on this book, my Mom told me it was from her good friend, Mary Wells. I have known Mary my entire life. She and her husband John have been friends of my parents since they first met in the young married Sunday School Class at Riverside Methodist. My Mom and Mary have shared the joys and comforts of true friendship through the years.

Lemon Pound Cake

1	cup shortening
3	cups flour
2	cups sugar
½	teaspoon salt
½	teaspoon soda
½	teaspoon baking powder
4	eggs
1	cup buttermilk
2	tablespoons lemon extract

Preheat oven to 325°. Grease and flour a bundt cake pan. Cream shortening and sugar. Mix other dry ingredients and add to sugar mixture. Add eggs and buttermilk. Beat until well mixed. Add extract and beat in. Bake 75 to 90 minutes. When done, let cool for 5 minutes then turn out on a plate. Glaze while hot.

Glaze:

2   cups powdered sugar
juice of one lemon or use 2
tablespoons of lemon juice

Combine powdered sugar with lemon juice and pour over hot cake. If necessary, return cake to oven for a few minutes until glaze melts.

Note: This is a wonderful cake to take to a church potluck or over to friends.

Herbert's Pound Cake

2	sticks butter
½	cup cooking oil
3	cups sugar
5	eggs
1½	teaspoons vanilla
3	cups flour
½	teaspoon baking powder
1	cup milk (regular)

Grease and flour a bundt cake pan. In a large mixing bowl, cream butter and oil. Add sugar and continue to cream. Add one egg at a time, beating after each egg. Add vanilla and mix well. Alternately, add combined dry ingredients and milk, mixing well after each addition. Be sure to end with the addition of dry ingredients. Pour batter into prepared bundt pan and place in a <u>cold</u> oven. DO NOT preheat oven. Cook at 350° for 75 minutes. Remove from oven and let cool before removing from pan.

Serving Suggestion: Wally served this with fresh strawberries and a scoop of vanilla ice cream. It was delicious!

My good friend, Wally Leaverton, served this wonderful cake at her son's birthday party. Once Dell and I tasted it I knew I had to have the recipe. Wally graciously obliged, but told me she got it from her father-in-law Herbert. I met Herbert and his wife Patricia when I was in college. Their son Clay was a friend of mine. They are two of the most gracious and kind people that I have ever met. Their hospitality is always warm and welcoming. After Wally and Clay married, we all kept in touch, and now our children attend the same school!

Cakes

A nice change of pace from your normal pound cake! This chocolate cake is wonderful like it is or with the glaze on page 147, for you chocolate lovers.

Serving suggestions: Slice and serve with a dollop of whipped topping and sliced strawberries. Chocolate dipped strawberries served on the side would also be yummy! See page 146 for instructions on making Chocolate Dipped Strawberries.

Chocolate Sour Cream Pound Cake

1	cup butter softened (2-sticks)
2	cups sugar
1	cup firmly packed brown sugar
6	large eggs
2½	cups all-purpose flour
½	teaspoon baking soda
½	cup cocoa
1	(8-ounce) carton sour cream
1	tablespoon vanilla
	powdered sugar (optional)

Preheat oven to 325°. Grease and flour a 10-inch tube pan. Beat softened butter until creamy. Gradually add sugars and blend for 3 minutes. Beat in eggs, one at a time. Combine flour, baking soda, and cocoa. Add dry mixture to creamed mixture alternating with sour cream. After each addition, mix at low speed just until blended. Stir in vanilla. Spoon batter into prepared tube pan. (Batter will be very thick.) Bake for 80 minutes or until toothpick comes out clean. Cool in pan on a wire rack for 10-15 minutes. Remove cake from pan and continue to cool on wire rack. If desired, sprinkle with powdered sugar.

Oatmeal Cake

1	cup oatmeal
1¼	cups boiling water
1	stick margarine
1	cup sugar
1	cup brown sugar
2	eggs
1⅓	cups sifted flour
1	teaspoon baking soda
1	teaspoon cinnamon

Preheat oven to 350°. Mix oatmeal and boiling water in a small bowl. Mix other ingredients in a large bowl. Combine ingredients from small and large bowls and bake in an oblong pan for 45 minutes.

Frosting:

1	stick margarine
1	cup brown sugar
1	cup coconut
1	cup chopped nuts
5	tablespoons cream or evaporated milk

In a medium sauce pan, heat ingredients over low heat until they bubble. Pour over cake while still hot.

I first met Ina May Stewart when I began frequenting her antique and gift store on 34th Street in Lubbock. Long before I met my husband, Dell, I loved to go in The Cottage. After I married Dell, I found out that his mother, Naydiene, and Ina May had been friends for years. They both belonged to the same garden club and shared a love of art, antiques, and good food! This Oatmeal Cake was her husband's favorite.

Cakes

Another wonderful recipe from my aunt, Bettye Jo Wiley. Aunt Bettye likes to use Bartlett Pears and enjoys making small size cakes to share with friends.

White Glaze:

1	tablespoon butter
2-3	tablespoons of reserved liquid from pears
1½	cups powdered sugar

Blend butter and powdered sugar with juice from pears. Use enough liquid to make a smooth, slightly thin frosting. Drizzle glaze over top of cooled cake, letting some run down the sides.

Fresh Pear Cake

2	cups firm fresh pears
1	cup sugar
3	cups sifted flour
1	teaspoon salt
1	teaspoon baking soda
1	teaspoon cinnamon
1⅓	cups salad oil
2	cups additional sugar
3	eggs
1	teaspoon vanilla
1	cup chopped pecans

Peel, core, and cut fresh pears into wedges. Add 1 cup of sugar to pears and cover with water. Cook 30 minutes or until tender. Drain well, reserving juice for glaze. Sift together flour, salt, soda, and cinnamon; set aside. Combine oil, sugar, eggs, and vanilla; beat well. Add flour mixture to creamed mixture. Fold in chopped pears and pecans. Spoon batter into a greased and floured 10-inch bundt or tube pan. Bake at 325° for 80 minutes or until cake tests done. Let cool in pan for 20 minutes and remove to cake rack for complete cooling. When cool, drizzle with White Glaze. (Recipe is in the side bar.)

Carrot Cake

2¼	cups all-purpose flour
1	teaspoon baking powder
2	teaspoons baking soda
1	teaspoon salt
2	teaspoons ground cinnamon
1⅓	cups granulated sugar
½	cup packed light or dark brown sugar
4	tablespoons (½ stick) butter, softened
1	cup vegetable oil
5	large eggs
3	cups coarsely shredded peeled raw carrots (6 medium)
1½	cups chopped pecans

Preheat oven to 350°. Grease and flour a 9x13-inch baking pan. Combine flour, baking powder, soda, salt, and cinnamon. In a large mixing bowl, cream both sugars and softened butter. Beat in oil until mixture is smooth. Add eggs, one at a time, and beat for 1 to 2 minutes or until mixture is thick and light. Blend in dry ingredients, then fold in the carrots and pecans. Spoon batter into prepared pan and bake for 50 to 60 minutes or until inserted toothpick comes out clean. When the cake is completely cool, generously ice with Cream Cheese Icing. (See next page)

Note: Keep this cake refrigerated. You may want to let pieces set out for a few minutes before serving.

I love Carrot Cake and Cream Cheese frosting! But I do not care for pineapple so this recipe is my favorite version. It is still moist and delicious. I like to bake it in a 9X13-inch pan because it is quick and easy. If you have time this makes a beautiful layer cake. Just frost in between the layers and on top. Sprinkle chopped pecans on top and enjoy!

Note: Toasting the pecans enhances their flavor. To toast spread the pecans on a jelly-roll pan and cook at 350° for 10 to 15 minutes stirring occasionally. Let them cool before stirring into the icing.

Cakes

This is my favorite icing! It is easy to make and is rich and delicious. It is also good on any type of spice or pumpkin cake.

Serve these beautiful chocolate dipped strawberries as a garnish beside chocolate cake, or on a pretty tray. Either way they are delicious!

It is only with gratitude that life becomes rich.

Cream Cheese Icing

1	(8-ounce) package cream cheese, softened
4	tablespoons butter
1	teaspoon vanilla
3 ½	cups powdered sugar, sifted

In a large mixing bowl, cream together cream cheese, butter, and vanilla. Gradually add the powdered sugar. Beat until creamy.

Chocolate Dipped Strawberries

24	large strawberries
1	cup semi-sweet chocolate chips
2	teaspoons shortening

Rinse whole strawberries leaving green tops on. Dry completely. (Chocolate will not stick to damp strawberries.) Line a cookie sheet with waxed paper. In a microwave-safe bowl, place chocolate chips and shortening. Microwave on high stirring every 30 seconds for 1 to 2 minutes until chocolate is melted. Dip half of each strawberry in melted chocolate. Place on wax paper. Once all strawberries are dipped refrigerate until chocolate is set.

Cakes

Vanilla Wafer Cake

2	cups sugar
6	eggs
2	sticks margarine, softened
1	(12-ounce) package vanilla wafers, crushed
½	cup chopped pecans
1	cup coconut

Cream sugar and margarine then add eggs; mix well. Add other ingredients and mix well. Butter a bundt pan then sprinkle with sugar instead of flour. Pour batter into prepared pan and bake in a 325° oven for 30 minutes. Reduce heat to 300° and bake for an additional 40 minutes.

Chocolate Glaze

1	tablespoon butter
2	tablespoons water
½	ounce unsweetened chocolate
1	cup powdered sugar
1	teaspoon vanilla

In a small saucepan, heat the butter, water, and chocolate over low heat. Stir until chocolate melts. Remove from heat and gradually stir in powdered sugar. Add vanilla and stir until mixture is smooth. Drizzle on cake of your choice.

Note: For extra flavor add ¼ teaspoon of ground cinnamon.

Another wonderful recipe from my friend, Claudine Youngblood. It is from her mother Ruth Grice Lewis. We all love the flavor of vanilla wafers and now you can have it in a slice of cake!

I placed this recipe here because I did not have room on the page with the Chocolate Pound Cake. When I did, I realized this glaze would be wonderful on the Vanilla Wafer Cake above! Try it for an extra-special treat!

147

Cakes

A friend of the family brought this to my mother-in law, Naydiene's house, when her husband Otis passed away. It was the most interesting cake she and I had ever seen! It looked like someone had dropped it or maybe not followed the recipe correctly. But when we tasted it, the cake was delicious. Naydiene and I always laughed about the way it looked. Years later I ran across a recipe for Upside Down German Chocolate Cake. The ingredients were almost identical. You simply turned the cake out so the good stuff on the bottom became the top!

Earthquake Cake

1	cup angel flake coconut
1	cup chopped pecans
1	(18.25-ounce) box German chocolate cake mix
3	large eggs
1¼	cups water
¼	cup vegetable oil
1	(8-ounce) package cream cheese, softened
1	(1-pound) box powdered sugar
1	stick margarine, melted

Spray a 9x13-inch pan with nonstick cooking spray. Combine pecans and coconut; sprinkle over bottom of pan. In a large bowl, combine cake mix, eggs, water, and oil. Mix according to package directions. Pour batter over coconut and pecan mixture. Whip cream cheese and melted butter together. Gradually stir in powdered sugar and mix until smooth. Spoon mixture over batter, spreading evenly. Bake in a preheated 350° oven for 45 minutes. Let cool on a wire rack for 10 minutes. Invert cake to serve.

Note: Some cooks suggest lining the pan with waxed paper first and then greasing the wax paper. This way the cake comes out easier and the topping doesn't stick to the bottom of the pan. Simply remove the waxed paper after the cake has been inverted and cooled.

Pam's Butter Cake

¼	cup shortening
1	cup sugar
2	eggs
1	cup flour
dash of salt	
1	teaspoon baking powder
½	cup milk
1	teaspoon vanilla

Grease and flour one round cake pan. Preheat oven to 325°. Place shortening in a mixing bowl and cream, continuing to add each ingredient. Mix until well blended. Pour in prepared pan and bake for 30 minutes.

To serve: Cut into 8 pie shape slices. Top with fresh sliced strawberries and fresh whipped cream.

Note: Pam sweetens the fresh cream with sugar as she whips it.

Helpful Hint: Cream will whip faster if the bowl and beaters are chilled.

Pam McPherson says this is one of her family's all-time favorites! Every time she serves it, everyone wants the recipe. Pam received the recipe from her great-grandmother, Annie Craig. The funny thing about the cake, is even though it is called Butter Cake, there is no butter in it. It doesn't matter though, because the cake is wonderfully moist and delicious!

Friends
are
God's life
preservers.

Cakes

*M*y husband, Dell, has been friends with the Harrist family for many years They farm near us and were very helpful to Dell when he first began farming. I met Phil and Shirley when Dell and I began dating. Actually Shirley's sister-in-law, Pam McPherson, (my "cousin" and good friend from college) set Dell and I up on our first date! A couple of years later, Phil Harrist was best man in our wedding! This recipe comes from his mother Edith. It is a wonderful rich chocolate cake that is enjoyed by the Harrist and McPherson families on birthdays and other special occasions.

Chocolate Dream Cake

2	cups sifted flour
2	cups sugar
½	cup margarine
½	cup shortening
1	cup water
¼	cup cocoa
½	cup buttermilk
2	eggs
1	teaspoon soda
1	teaspoon vanilla

Place sifted flour and sugar in a large mixing bowl. Bring margarine, shortening, and water to a boil. Pour in with flour/sugar mixture. Beat with mixer until well blended. Combine buttermilk, eggs, soda, and vanilla. Add to batter and mix until well blended and creamy. Pour into a 9 X 13-inch baking pan that has been greased with shortening. Bake at 400° for 35 to 40 minutes. Cool for 15 minutes then pour on frosting.

It is one of the most beautiful compensations of this life that no man can sincerely try to help another without helping himself.

Chocolate Dream Frosting

1	stick margarine
3½	tablespoons cocoa
⅓	cup milk
⅓	cup chopped pecans
1	teaspoon vanilla
1	(1-pound) package powdered sugar

In a medium-size saucepan combine margarine, cocoa, and milk. Bring to a boil. Remove from heat and stir in pecans and vanilla. Gradually beat in powdered sugar. Mix until well blended and creamy. Pour over warm cake.

Note: As soon as you take the Chocolate Dream Cake out of the oven to cool, begin to make the frosting. By the time you have made the frosting the cake will have cooled for the 15 minutes. Pour the frosting on the warm cake. This frosting kind of melts down into the cake. The results are incredibly delicious!!

Cakes

The frosting is what makes the Chocolate Dream cake on the previous page so incredible. Pour it on after the cake has cooled for 15 minutes, for a dream of a cake!

Note: If you buy powdered sugar in bulk. The equivalent of 1 pound is 3 ¾ cups unsifted.

Friendship is a sheltering tree.

Cakes

I *met Lynn and Sue Haney in 1982 when we first showed our products at the Dallas Market. We have all come a long way and many things have changed since those early days! Lynn is now famous for his beautiful Santas. It has been fun to watch their business grow. Most importantly, their success has not changed them. They are still both the same friendly caring people they were when I first met them. Through it all they have remembered that the most important things in life are not things, but family and friends.*

Applesauce Cake

3	cups flour
2	teaspoons baking soda
½	teaspoon salt
½	teaspoon cinnamon
½	teaspoon ground cloves
½	teaspoon nutmeg
1½	cups chopped pecans
1	cup raisins
1	cup sugar
½	cup butter
1	egg
1½	cups applesauce
4	tablespoons hot water

Sift flour with soda, salt, and spices. Mix in pecans and raisins; toss to coat. In a large mixing bowl, cream sugar and butter. Add egg and beat well. Stir in applesauce. Add 4 tablespoons hot water to mixture. Add flour mixture to butter and apple-sauce mixture. Mix together, taking care not to over mix. Bake in a bundt or tube pan at 250° for 1 hour or until toothpick comes out clean from the center. Cool on wire rack before removing from the cake pan.

Serving Suggestion: Sue said this cake is delicious when served warm with butter. It is also wonderful to serve with coffee or tea.

Rosemary's Apple Candy Pie

1	frozen apple pie

Topping:

4	tablespoons butter
½	cup brown sugar, firmly packed
2	tablespoons milk or cream
½	cup chopped pecans

Bake frozen pie according to package directions. (Note: Be sure to place it on a cookie sheet so it won't bake over in your oven.) Prepare topping by melting butter in a saucepan, stir in brown sugar and milk or cream. Heat to boiling. Remove from heat. Add pecans. Spread over top of pie. Return pie to oven and bake 5 minutes longer or until top bubbles.

Note: Rosemary likes to use the Plush Pippin brand of frozen pie.

If you like to make your own apple pie that is great too. Just try this topping on your freshly baked pie for an extra special touch!

My cousin, Rosemary West, who is a wonderful cook, gave me this delicious and incredibly easy recipe. She said it is wonderful when you need a quick "homemade" dessert to take to someone. The smell of hot apple pie is always warm and welcoming.

Serving suggestion: Add a scoop of your favorite vanilla ice cream to each slice for a scrumptious dessert!

A friend loves at all times.

Proverbs 17:17

153

Pies

Beverly Bird served this pie years ago at a gathering of friends. As soon as I tasted it I knew I had to have the recipe! I never got around to it until I began working on this book, so I sent her a note. She e-mailed the recipe and couldn't believe I remembered having this pie. I told her when something is that good I never forget! Besides, it combines several of my favorites; caramel, cream cheese, and toasted coconut. She also told me it wasn't her recipe, but it was Jane Evans. Thank you Jane and Beverly for sharing this wonderful recipe!

Jane's Coconut Caramel Pie

2	prepared graham cracker crusts

Filling:

1	(8-ounce) package cream cheese, softened
1	can sweetened condensed milk
1	(12-ounce) carton frozen whipped topping, thawed
1	jar caramel ice cream topping
1	(7-ounce) package coconut, toasted

Combine cream cheese, milk, and whipped topping; blend until smooth. Fill graham cracker crusts with mixture. Top with caramel then sprinkle with toasted coconut. Place in freezer until ready to serve.

To toast coconut: Spread coconut in a single layer on a baking sheet with sides. Bake at 325°, stirring occasionally, for approximately 10 minutes or until golden brown.

Caramel Coconut Pie

1	can sweetened condensed milk
1	(8-ounce) package cream cheese, softened
1	(10-ounce) carton frozen whipped topping, thawed
¼	cup margarine
½	cup chopped pecans
¾	cup coconut
2	baked pie shells
1	jar caramel ice cream topping

Blend sweetened condensed milk, softened cream cheese, and whipped topping together until smooth. Melt margarine in a medium sauce pan and add pecans and coconut. Stir pecans and coconut in butter over medium heat until golden brown. Spread a layer of cream filling in bottom of pie shells. Top with coconut and pecan mixture. Drizzle with caramel. Fill pie shells with remaining cream filling and once again top with coconut-pecan mixture and caramel. Place in freezer.

This pie is similar to the recipe on the previous page except it uses a regular pie crust and adds pecans. I received this scrumptious recipe from Eva Dean Stephens. Her daughter Kendra was my son Logan's fifth grade teacher. Have you ever met someone and instantly knew you would be friends? That is the way I felt the first time I met Kendra and then later when I met her mother, Eva Dean. We have shared joys, sorrows, faith and hope, and through it all a love for family and friends.

Pies

*P*aula Johnson's
sister Donna Walker,
makes this wonderful
pie. Paula also makes
it often because it is
delicious and easy to
make! The Butter
Crunch crust adds to
the richness of the pie.

*T*his recipe makes
2 pie crusts. It is also a
good quick crust recipe
to make for any cream
pie or dessert.

Aunt Donna's Blueberry Banana Pie

2	Butter Crunch pie crusts
1	(8-ounce) package cream cheese
½	cup powdered sugar
1	(12-ounce) carton whipped topping
3-4	ripe bananas, sliced
1	(16-ounce) can blueberry pie filling

Cream powdered sugar and cream cheese together. On low speed, mix in whipped topping. Layer on top of each cooled crust the following: sliced bananas, cream cheese mixture, and pie filling. Refrigerate until ready to serve.

Butter Crunch Crust

1	stick margarine, room temperature
4	tablespoons brown sugar
1	cup flour
½	cup chopped pecans

Preheat oven to 400°. Mix all ingredients with hands. Crumble into oblong cake pan. Bake approximately 15 minutes, stirring often. Crust is ready when it begins to brown and is dry and crumbly. (Note: Watch closely to prevent it from burning.) Remove from oven. Working quickly, separate mixture into small crumbles with a fork. Press into two, 9-inch pie plates while still warm. Cool and fill.

Chocolate Silk Pie

½	cup butter, softened
¾	cup sugar
2	(1-ounce) squares unsweetened chocolate, melted
1	teaspoon vanilla
2	eggs
1	graham cracker crust
1	(10-ounce) carton frozen whipped topping, thawed

Beat butter until fluffy, beat in sugar. Add melted chocolate and vanilla. Beat in eggs, one at a time, beating 3 minutes each. Fill pie shell and refrigerate for 2 hours. Top with whipped topping and chocolate curls.

To make chocolate curls: Slightly soften a 3 to 4 inch bar of chocolate. You can do this in the microwave on medium (50 % power) or, you can simply bring the chocolate bar to room temperature. Using a vegetable peeler create curls by paring the side of the chocolate bar. Refrigerate curls until ready to use.

Pies

*P*am McPherson served this yummy pie one summer as we all vacationed in the cool Colorado mountains. Pam and I took turns cooking each night. It was great fun and gave us a chance to swap recipes. This is one of Pam's recipes that she got from her friend and former neighbor Donna Cox.

My best friend is the one that brings out the best in me.

Pies

Ginny Huddleston
Secor sent this classic
family favorite, Ginny's
relatives live in
Murfreesboro, TN. and
are all wonderful cooks.

Chocolate Chess Pie

2	squares unsweetened chocolate
½	cup butter
1½	cups sugar
⅓	cup milk
2	eggs slightly beaten
⅛	teaspoon salt
1	teaspoon vanilla

Melt chocolate and butter in a double boiler or microwave. Take off heat and add remaining ingredients. Pour into an uncooked 9-inch pie shell. In a preheated 350° oven, cook for 40-50 minutes.

Helpful hint from Ginny: It is difficult to tell when a chess pie is done, because it often doesn't set up completely until it cools. "I usually cook it until a 1-inch ring around the edge is firm."

A good
old-fashion favorite!
Martha McCormick, a
friend of my family's
from Keller, sent us this
family recipe. She said
it is her daughter Lisa's
favorite!

Buttermilk Pie

3	whole eggs, well beaten
2	cups sugar mixed with 3 tablespoons flour
½	cup butter, melted
1	cup buttermilk
1	teaspoon vanilla

Mix all ingredients with mixer. Pour into an unbaked 9-inch pie shell. Bake in a preheated 325° oven for 60 minutes or until pie sets.

Coconut Pineapple Pie

1	stick margarine, melted
1	(5-ounce) can evaporated milk
1½	cups sugar
3	eggs
1	(15-ounce) can crushed pineapple
1	(7-ounce) can flaked coconut
1	tablespoon vinegar
1	teaspoon vanilla
1	(9-inch) pie shell, unbaked

Combine all ingredients and pour into an unbaked pie shell. Bake for 60 minutes in a preheated 350˚ oven.

The glory of a friendship is not the outstretched hand, nor the kindly smile, nor the joy of companionship. It is the spiritual inspiration that comes to one when he discovers that someone else believes in him and is willing to trust him with his friendship.

Ralph Waldo Emerson

A good friend from college, Cissy Doran Mobley, gave me this recipe. She and her roommate Claudia were Kappas and were like "big sisters" to me. She said this was their favorite pie. Cissy now lives in College Station, Texas, home of Texas Tech's arch rival those A&M Aggies! I was scheduled to speak at a church in Bryan/ College Station last fall when I received a phone call from Cissy. She did not attend that church anymore, but was teaching a Bible study there. She saw that I was coming and arranged to attend. I was delighted to see her again and "catch up" over lunch.

Pies

*T*he first time I had this pie was in the dorm at Texas Tech. It was really good. One of the best things about dorm food were the desserts! I was a member of a sorority, but my roommate and most of my friends in the dorm were not. My cousin Donna lived on the same floor. Every time they served this pie her roommate "Reeser" (aka Theresa) would put a note on my dorm door. She thought those of us in sororities would like it because it was called "Mystic" pie. She loved to tease us about our sorority "secrets". Actually the only mystery about the pie to most people is what it is made of.

Mystic Pie

4	egg whites
1	cup sugar
20	Ritz crackers, finely crushed
½	cup chopped nuts
½	teaspoon baking powder

Grease an 8-inch pie pan. Preheat oven to 350°. Beat egg whites until stiff. Add sugar to egg whites and beat until dry. Fold in nuts, crackers and baking powder. Bake for 30 minutes. Cool pie completely before serving.

Helpful Hint: If you have a wire whisk attachment for your mixer use it to beat the egg whites. It makes this process so much easier.

Serving Suggestion: This pie is delicious served with a dollop of whipped topping.

It was chance that made us sisters, but our hearts made us friends.

Peanut Butter Silk Pie

1	(9-inch) prepared chocolate cookie crumb pie crust
1	(8-ounce) cream cheese, softened
1	cup sugar
1	cup creamy peanut butter
1	tablespoon butter or margarine, melted
1	teaspoon vanilla extract
1	cup heavy whipping cream, beaten until stiff

Beat cream cheese, sugar, peanut butter, butter, and vanilla together. Gently fold in whipped cream. Pour into pie shell. Spread topping over pie and chill uncovered for 1 hour or until topping is firm. Then loosely cover and refrigerate over night.

Topping:

1	cup semisweet chocolate chips
3	tablespoons brewed coffee

Combine chocolate chips and coffee in a microwave safe bowl. Heat on high for 1½ to 2 minutes or until chocolate is melted. Stir ½ way through.

Note: You can garnish the pie with chopped peanuts if desired.

Another delicious recipe from Cissy Mobley. (Actually she now goes by her given name Corrine, but I have known her since college and she will always be Cissy to me). This recipe combines two of my favorites; chocolate and peanut butter!

I thank my God every time I remember you.

Phil. 1:3

Pies

Cissy also gave me this recipe. It's out of a cookbook from the church where I was speaking; First Baptist in Bryan. One evening while I was there, we had pie and coffee after I spoke. Cissy told me about this recipe and said that the butternut flavoring added an extra special taste to the pie. I was delighted when she brought me this recipe the next day at lunch. My time in Bryan/ College Station was extra special because of the warm hospitality from all of the ladies at First Baptist and the time spent with Cissy, renewing our friendship!

Texas Pecan Pie

⅓	cup butter, melted
1	cup sugar
1	cup white corn syrup
½	teaspoon salt
4	eggs
1	teaspoon vanilla extract
1	teaspoon vanilla, butternut extract
1	cup chopped pecans
1	unbaked pie shell

Combine butter, sugar, syrup, and salt. Slightly beat eggs and add to mixture. Add extract and pecans. Pour mixture into an unbaked pie shell and bake in a preheated 350° oven for 40 to 50 minutes.

Note: You will have to get the butternut flavoring from your local Watkins distributor. It's worth the effort to get the flavoring because it is what makes this pecan pie extra-special!

French Cherry Pie

Crust:

3	egg whites
1	teaspoon vinegar
1	cup sugar
1	teaspoon vanilla extract
1	teaspoon baking powder
12	soda crackers, coarsely crushed
½	cup pecans, chopped

Beat egg whites with 1 teaspoon of vinegar until stiff. Slowly add sugar into egg whites while beating. Add vanilla then stir in baking powder. Fold in crackers and pecans. Spread in the bottom of a 9x11-inch pan and bake for 20 minutes in a 325° oven.

Filling:

1	(16-ounce) can cherry pie filling
1	(3-ounce) cream cheese
½	cup powdered sugar
1	cup whipping cream
1½	teaspoons vanilla

Whip cream until stiff and add vanilla. Cream the cream cheese and powdered sugar then fold into whipped cream. Pour over baked crust. Mix cherry pie filling with 1 teaspoon of vanilla extract (this enhances the cherry flavor) then spread cherries over top of cream mixture. Chill five hours before serving.

Billie Jeane Garner sent us this beautiful cherry pie recipe. It is from her friend Jerri Dunn. Jerri has made this pie every year for over 40 years for her husband's birthday, because it is his favorite!

A true friend laughs at your stories even when they're not so good, and sympathizes with your troubles even when they are not so bad.

This is our version of a wonderful pie also sent to us by Billie Jeane Garner. The combination of berries makes a colorful and refreshing pie. You can reduce the calorie content by using a lowfat pie crust, and substituting sugar-free jello and Splenda for the sugar. Either way this pie is sure to be a favorite during the summer when fresh berries are abundant!

Friends are like two clocks keeping time together.

Summer Berry Pie

1	graham cracker pie crust
¾	cup sugar
3	tablespoons cornstarch
1½	cups water
1	(3-ounce) package raspberry or strawberry jello
1½	cups fresh raspberries
1½	cups sliced fresh strawberries
1	cup fresh blueberries
½	(8-ounce) carton frozen whipped topping

In a medium sauce pan, combine sugar and cornstarch. Slowly stir in water. Cook over low heat stirring until smooth. Increase heat to medium and cook for 1 minute after it boils. Remove from heat and stir in dry jello until dissolved. Cool to room temperature. Mix washed and drained berries together and pour into pie shell. Pour cooled jello mixture over berries. Refrigerate for at least 30 minutes. Spread whipped topping over berries and garnish with additional berries.

Yield: 6 servings

Reba's Chocolate Pie

Pies

2	cups milk
3 or 4	egg yolks, slightly beaten (save whites for meringue)
2	cups sugar
4	rounded tablespoons flour
2	teaspoons cocoa
3	tablespoons butter
1	tablespoon pure vanilla extract
	dash of salt

In a heavy saucepan, combine milk, sugar, flour, and cocoa. Heat mixture over medium heat until hot. Quickly add egg yolks, stirring briskly all the while. Cook mixture, stirring until it is very thick. Remove from heat and add butter, vanilla, and salt. Mix well. Pour into a baked pie crust, top with meringue and brown in a 325° oven for 30 minutes.

Never Fail Meringue:

1	tablespoon cornstarch
2	tablespoons boiling water
3 or 4	egg whites
6	tablespoons sugar
1	teaspoon vanilla
	pinch of salt

Mix cornstarch with 2 tablespoons cold water in a saucepan. Add boiling water and cook over medium heat, stirring constantly, until mixture is clear and thickened. *Let stand until completely cold.* With electric mixer, beat egg whites until foamy. Gradually add sugar and beat until stiff, but not dry. Reduce speed to low, add vanilla and salt. Gradually beat in cold cornstarch mixture. Return mixer to high speed and beat well. Spread meringue over cooled pie filling and bake in a 325° oven for approximately 30 minutes.

Reba McPherson is known for her pies. Reba is the mother of our dear friends Shirley Harrist and Rick McPherson. Throughout their lives they have enjoyed her wonderful pies. Shirley also said that Reba's pies are the first desserts to vanish at church fellowships!

Note: Reba saves time by cooking the cornstarch before making the pie filling, that way it will be cool enough when time to make the meringue. It is also important not to rush browning the meringue.

Another of Reba McPherson's famous pies! Her pies have comforted the sick and those that are grieving. They have welcomed new babies as well as, visitors. Shirley shared that since she and her brother Rick married and have families of their own, Reba's pies are always part of their holiday dinners. The grandchildren are always glad to see "Memaw's" car in the driveway because they know they can look forward to one of her delicious pies!

Reba's Coconut Pie

1	cooked pie shell
4	eggs
¾	cup evaporated milk
1	cup sugar
4	rounded tablespoons flour
¾	cup water
3	tablespoons margarine
½	teaspoon vanilla
¼	teaspoon coconut flavoring

In a saucepan, beat egg yolks then stir in milk and water. Stirring well, gradually add sugar and flour. Cook mixture over medium-low heat until it thickens. Take off the burner and add margarine, vanilla, coconut flavoring, and a pinch of salt. Beat until smooth and creamy. Pour into cooked pie shell. Top with meringue and sprinkle with coconut. Bake at 325° until lightly browned.

Note: See previous page for Reba's Never-Fail meringue.

Crust: Combine 2 cups flour, 1 teaspoon salt, ⅔ cup shortening and 5 to 6 tablespoons of cold water. Mix together and roll out to fit pie pan. Bake at 400° until brown.

Note: Reba's daughter-in-law, Pam McPherson, likes to use her hand mixer to beat the pie until it is real creamy and fluffy. Pam also shared that Reba said if you do not have evaporated milk use regular milk and no water.

Pink Surprise Lemonade Pie

1   (8-ounce) carton whipped
     topping
1   (6-ounce) can pink lemonade,
     thawed until it is slushy
1   (14-ounce) can sweetened
     condensed milk
1   graham cracker crust

Mix all ingredients together with mixer until smooth. Freeze and serve.

Another delicious recipe from Pam McPherson. This recipe came from her grandmother Gladys Young. It is easy to make and very refreshing on a hot summer day.

Graham Cracker Crust

1¼   cups graham cracker crumbs
¼   cup sugar
⅓   cup margarine, melted

Combine graham cracker crumbs and sugar. Add melted margarine and stir until mixed. Press crumb mixture firmly into a lightly greased pie pan. It helps to use the back of a spoon to press the crumbs up the side and onto the bottom of the pie pan. Bake at 375° for 6 to 8 minutes. Cool completely and then fill. Note: If you are making a refrigerated or frozen pie you don't have to bake the crust. Simply freeze crust 5 to 10 minutes before filling.

Note: You can purchase a ready made graham cracker crust but, Pam says it's better if you make your own!

A time saving tip from Pam: Purchase the already crushed graham cracker crumbs at your local grocery store.

Pies

The crust on this ice cream pie adds an extra crunch and rich chocolate flavor to an already decadent pie. If you love caramel and chocolate, this one is sure to be a favorite. Top it with a little wipped topping and chopped pecans for a treat better than an ice cream sundae.
This pie is also easy to make!

Caramel Chocolate Chip Ice Cream Pie

½ cup chocolate syrup
⅓ cup semisweet chocolate chips
2 cups crisp rice cereal
1 quart chocolate chip ice cream, softened
1 (12-ounce) jar caramel ice cream sauce

Lightly grease an 8-inch pie pan with butter. In a small microwave safe bowl, combine chocolate syrup and chocolate chips. Microwave on high about 30 seconds, stir and cook another 15 seconds. Stir until smooth. Reserve ¼ cup of chocolate mixture. In a medium bowl, pour remaining chocolate mixture over cereal. Stir until well coated. Press mixture into pie pan, covering bottom and up the sides. Freeze until firm, about 20 minutes. Spread half the ice cream in prepared crust. Pour on ¾ of the caramel sauce. Top with remaining ice cream. Smooth top of pie. Drizzle with remaining caramel and chocolate sauce. Cover and freeze for at least one hour or until firm.

Note: If you would prefer you can use vanilla ice cream or experiment with your favorite flavor. For a quick and easy pie, fill the chocolate crust with carmel chocolate pecan ice cream. This way the toppings are already mixed in!

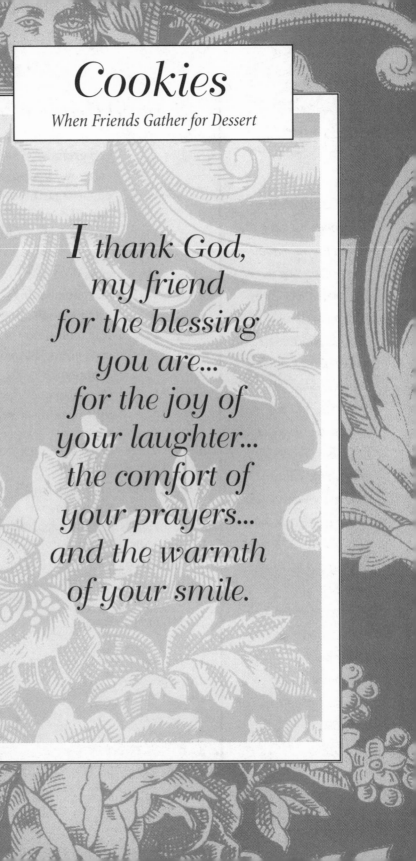

Cookies

When Friends Gather for Dessert

*I thank God,
my friend
for the blessing
you are...
for the joy of
your laughter...
the comfort of
your prayers...
and the warmth
of your smile.*

Almond Crunch Cookies

1	cup granulated sugar
1	cup powdered sugar
1	cup margarine, softened
1	cup oil
1	teaspoon almond extract
2	eggs
4½	cups flour
1	teaspoon baking soda
1	teaspoon salt
1	teaspoon cream of tartar
2	cups almonds, coarsely chopped
1	(6-ounce) package almond toffee baking bits

Blend sugar, powdered sugar, margarine, and oil. Add extract and eggs. Mix well. On low speed, gradually blend in flour, baking soda, salt, and cream of tartar. Stir in almonds and toffee bits. Shape into balls. Place on ungreased cookie sheet. Flatten with a fork and bake at 350° for 12 minutes or until light brown around the edges.

Yield: 7 dozen or more

Serving Suggestion: This is a great cookie to serve with coffee or tea.

*C*arol Witt shared this wonderful cookie recipe. I have made these often, and everyone loves them! They are not too sweet...sort of like a shortbread cookie. Everyone tries to guess what the crunch is, and are surprised to find out it is toffee bits! I met Carol, through my cousin, Rosemary West. Carol began working at All Seasons in 1977 after starting out there as one of Rosemary's painting students. Carol is a wonderful cook! Check out her Raspberry Cream Cheese Coffee Cake on page 39.

Buffalo Chip Cookies

2	cups butter or margarine
2	cups brown sugar
2	cups white sugar
4	eggs
2	teaspoons vanilla extract
4	cups flour
2	teaspoons baking powder
2	cups oatmeal
2	cups corn flakes, crushed
2	cups pecans, chopped
1	(6-ounce) package chocolate chips
½	package chocolate chunks

Melt butter and let cool. In a large bowl, mix butter with sugars, eggs, and vanilla. Sift in flour, soda, and baking powder. Add remaining ingredients and combine. Scoop with an ice cream scoop and place on a greased cookie sheet. Bake at 350° for 15 minutes. You can make smaller cookies and adjust cooking time.

Note: My sister uses a muffin scoop instead of an ice cream scoop.

A West family favorite! Rosemary West always brings this scrumptious cookie to family gatherings.

Note: The secret is to not rush the process. You must let the butter cool. Also put the dough in the freezer or refrigerator and let it thoroughly chill before scooping out the cookies.

Helpful Hint: Rosemary also scoops the cookies out and then freezes them. This way she can have fresh warm cookies at a moments notice.

A wonderfully light cookie! Perfect for bridal or baby showers. The name describes them best ....they will melt in your mouth!

Hint: Tint the icing to match the bride-to-be's colors, or the nursery colors for an expectant mother. Also you can leave out the lemon juice and use milk to mix your icing. Add the flavoring of your choice such as vanilla or almond extract.

Melting Moments

⅔   **cup unsifted cornstarch**
⅓   **cup unsifted powdered sugar**
1   **cup flour**
1   **cup butter, softened**

Sift flour and cornstarch together. Cream sugar and butter, add flour and cornstarch. Drop by rounded teaspoons on an ungreased cookie sheet. Bake at 350° for about 15 minutes or until lightly browned. Check after 10 minutes. Do not over cook.

Icing:

¼   **cup butter, room temperature**
2   **teaspoons grated lemon rind**
2   **tablespoons fresh lemon juice**
3   **cups powdered sugar**

Combine butter, lemon juice and lemon rind. Mix in powdered sugar. (Icing will be stiff). Spread icing on cookies.

Yield: 4 dozen cookies

Hidden Kisses

1	cup butter, softened
½	cup powdered sugar (plus extra for rolling)
1	teaspoon vanilla
2	cups all-purpose flour
1	cup finely chopped pecans
1	(9-ounce) package chocolate kisses

Preheat oven to 375°. Cream butter. Add ½ cup powdered sugar and vanilla. Beat on low until light and fluffy. Add flour and pecans. Shape small portions of dough around each unwrapped kiss. Bake on an ungreased, air-cushion cookie sheet for 12 minutes or until lightly browned. Let cool for 10 minutes; then roll in powdered sugar.

Yield: 40 to 45 cookies

Note: I like to use the chocolate kisses with almonds for an extra-special taste!

Hepful Hint: Before you mix up the dough, unwrap 40 to 45 of the chocolate kisses. This will make the process go a lot faster and easier!

You will be pleasantly surprised when you bite into this cookie! Hidden inside is a chocolate surprise. My cousin, Carol West Wheeler, shared this delightful cookie recipe.

Note: If you don't let these cool before you roll in powdered sugar, the sugar will melt into the cookie. I find it easier to put the powdered sugar in a shallow bowl and dip the top side of each cookie after they have cooled.

173

*M*y sister, Karen Franks, loves to serve these cookies. They are wonderful for baby showers or any special occasion.

*Y*ou can tint the icing to match the colors you are using. So many mothers-to-be now know if they are having a boy or a girl. While blue icing is not very appetizing you can ice the cookies with white or yellow and then accent with blue polka dots or stripes. Have fun and be creative! Look for baby themed cookie cutters at your local cooking store.

174

Karen's Old Fashion Rolled Sugar Cookies

6	cups sifted all-purpose flour
2	cups sugar
3	teaspoons baking powder
1	teaspoon salt
2	cups butter or margarine, softened
2	eggs, slightly beaten
6	tablespoons heavy cream
2	teaspoons vanilla extract

Preheat oven to 400°. Sift flour with sugar, baking powder, and salt into a mixing bowl. Cut in butter with mixer or pastry blender until particles are fine. Add egg, cream, and vanilla. Blend thoroughly. If desired chill dough for at least 1 hour for easier handling. Roll out on floured surface ⅓ at a time to a thickness of ⅛ of an inch. Sprinkle with sugar and cut into shapes. Bake on an ungreased cookie sheet for 5 to 8 minutes

Icing:

½	cup butter
½	cup vegetable shortening
½	teaspoon vanilla extract
3	tablespoons milk
1	(1-pound) box powdered sugar

Cream butter and shortening; add vanilla and milk. Gradually add powdered sugar and beat until smooth and creamy.

Butterscotch Cookies

1	cup butter
2	cups brown sugar
2	teaspoons vanilla extract
2	eggs
3½	cups flour, sifted
3	teaspoons baking powder
1	cup chopped pecans

Using a mixer, cream butter and brown sugar. Add vanilla and beat in eggs, one at a time. Stir in flour that has been sifted with the baking powder. Mix thoroughly. If desired, add the chopped pecans. Make into 3 long rolls that are about 2 inches in diameter. Wrap tightly in waxed paper. Refrigerate for a few hours (or up to 5 days). Slice and bake on ungreased cookie sheet. Bake at 375° for 10 to 12 minutes. Do not brown.

Note: You can also freeze extra rolls in ziplock bags. Simply place in refrigerator to thaw the night before you plan to bake more cookies.

*A*nn Adams, a sweet friend from Tahoka, sent me this recipe. Both Dell and I remember our mothers making "refrigerator cookies" when we were kids. Ann enclosed a cute story with the recipe. Once when her son, Phil, was a teenager and home alone for awhile, he decided to bake some cookies from the roll Ann had in the refrigerator. When she got home he said, "Mother, I tried to bake some cookies, but they just burned and got the oven dirty!" Ann soon realized he had place the cookies directly on to the oven rack. Phil had always seen warm cookies cooling on a rack in the kitchen!

A delightful new recipe! Every time I make these I can hardly keep up with the demand. My son Logan and his friends eat these by the handful! If your family does not like peanuts, substitute peanut butter cups. My daughter, Kaitlyn , prefers them this way. Either way you have a crowd pleaser!

It's your love your friends need- not expensive gifts or extravagant surprises.

Peanut Butter Surprise

1	cup butter, softened
1	cup peanut butter
1	cup sugar
1	cup light brown sugar, firmly packed
2	large eggs
2	teaspoons vanilla
3½	cups all-purpose flour
1	teaspoon baking powder
1	teaspoon baking soda
½	teaspoon salt
2	(13-ounce) packages of miniature Snickers

Cream butter and peanut butter; gradually add sugars. Add eggs and vanilla, beat mixture well. Combine flour, baking powder, soda, and salt. Gradually add flour mixture to butter mixture, beating just until blended. Cover and refrigerate for at least 2 hours. Unwrap candy squares. Using approximately 1 tablespoon of dough, wrap around each piece of candy. Roll in your hand to round and smooth. Place on an ungreased cookie sheet. Bake in a preheated, 350° oven for 12 to 15 minutes or until cookies are lightly browned. Let cool 10 minutes before serving.

Yield: 6-8 dozen cookies If you don't wrap too much dough around the candy you can get up to 8 dozen cookies.

Oatmeal Crisps

1	cup vegetable oil
1	cup brown sugar
1	cup granulated sugar
2	eggs beaten
1	teaspoon vanilla
4	cups quick cooking oats
1	cup flour
½	teaspoon salt
1	teaspoon soda
1	cup chopped pecans
1	cup coconut

Mix oil and sugars. Add eggs and vanilla. Beat until fluffy. Stir together oats, flour, salt, and baking soda. Stir oat mixture into beaten mixture, blending well. Stir in pecans and coconut. Shape into 1-inch balls. Bake in a preheated 350° oven for 10 to 12 minutes.

Yield: 4 dozen

Sharing recipes was as much a part of All Seasons as sharing painting ideas. Good food was always part of the painting classes. This delightful oatmeal cookie recipe is from one of All Seasons' customers. I like these oatmeal cookies because they are both crunchy and chewy!

The way to be happy is to make others happy.

177

I met Patsy Kincaid at the Dallas Market the first year I was marketing my cookbook "Where Hearts Gather". I was still new to the cookbook marketing business, and Patsy had helped market the highly successful "Celebrate San Antonio" cookbook. I will always remember and be thankful for her words of wisdom and encouragement! Patsy began making this recipe for her daughter Holly's swim class. Later Holly attended school in California and played water polo. When Patsy went to visit her, if she got off the plane without these cookies, the girls on the polo team would, jokingly, tell her to go back home!

178

Aunt Elsie's Oatmeal Cookies

1	cup vegetable shortening
2	cups brown sugar, packed
⅓	cup milk
2	eggs, beaten
3	cups oatmeal (3 Minute or rolled oats)
3	cups flour
2	teaspoons baking powder
2	teaspoons baking soda
1	teaspoon cinnamon
½	teaspoon salt
¼	teaspoon ground cloves
1	cup raisins

In a large mixing bowl, cream together shortening and brown sugar. Add milk and eggs; mix well. In a separate bowl combine oatmeal, flour, baking powder, soda, cinnamon, salt and cloves. Combine dry mixture with wet mixture and mix well. Mix in raisins. Drop on a slightly greased cookie sheet and bake in a 400° oven for 8 to 10 minutes.

Yield: 6 dozen

Note: Patsy got this recipe when she was about 9 years old from her Aunt Elsie. She has made them for years!

Butter Cookies

½   cup butter
½   cup shortening
1   cup sugar
3   eggs
3½   cups all-purpose flour
2   teaspoons cream of tartar
1   teaspoon soda
1½   teaspoons vanilla extract
decorator sugar crystals

Cream butter and shortening, gradually add sugar. Beat until light and fluffy. Add eggs, one at a time; beat well after each addition. Sift together flour, cream of tartar, and soda. Gradually add dry ingredients to creamed mixture. Add vanilla and mix well. This is a very thick dough. You may need to finish stirring by hand. Chill dough 2 hours. Roll out on a lightly floured work surface to ¼ inch thickness. Cut out with cookie cutters. Place on an ungreased cookie sheet. Sprinkle with sugar crystals or leave plain if you are going to ice them. Bake at 425° for 6 to 8 minutes or until lightly browned.

Yield: 3 dozen large cookies or 5½ dozen
        smaller cookies

Note: For best results use metal cookie cutters and bake the cookies on air-cushion cookie sheets.

This is my favorite cookie recipe to use with cookie cutters. It has a wonderful flavor, and the cookies are easy to cut out. I often use it at Valentine's. You can either sprinkle with red sugar crystals or ice with your favorite icing.

My favorite icing recipe is as follows: Cream together ½ cup shortening and ½ cup of butter. Gradually add 3¾ cup unsifted powdered sugar alternately with 3 tablespoons of milk and 1 teaspoon of vanilla. Mix on medium speed until creamy.

Hearts are one of my favorites. They are also part of many of the painting patterns at All Seasons. This is another delicious cookie from their Open House recipe booklet. These would be great for Valentine's Day or a special anniversary celebration!

Nothing
the heart
gives away
is gone,
it is kept
in the hearts
of others.

Stenciled Gingerbread Hearts

1	cup shortening
1	cup molasses
3	cups all-purpose flour
2	teaspoons baking soda
½	teaspoon salt
½	teaspoon ginger
¼	teaspoon nutmeg
¼	teaspoon cloves

milk
powdered sugar

In a large bowl, combine shortening and molasses; blend well. Add flour, baking soda, salt, ginger, nutmeg, and cloves to molasses mixture. Mix well. Cover with plastic wrap and refrigerate for 2 hours. Preheat oven to 350°. Roll dough about ¼ inch thick on a well floured surface. Cut with heart shaped cookie cutter. Place 1-inch apart on an ungreased cookie sheet. Bake for 8 to 10 minutes or until set. Remove from cookie sheet and cool. Brush cookies lightly with milk. Press stencil or paper doily down over cookie. Using a wire strainer, sprinkle evenly with powdered sugar. Carefully remove doily or stencil.

Sugar Cookies

1	cup confectioners' sugar
1	cup sugar
2	sticks butter
1	cup shortening
2	eggs
2	teaspoons vanilla
1/8	teaspoon salt
4 1/2	cups flour
1 1/8	teaspoons soda
1 1/8	teaspoons cream of tartar

Combine ingredients in order. Refrigerate 1 hour; then roll into small balls. Press onto greased baking sheet, using a glass dipped in water and then in sugar. Bake at 375° for 8 to 10 minutes.

Note: For fun try the colored or sparkling sugars available at gourmet or cooking stores. Or try the following flavored sugars:

Vanilla sugar: Make your own by placing two vanilla beans in a pound of granulated sugar for at least a week. Store at room temperature in an air-tight container. Stir mixture once or twice. After one week, remove the beans. The sugar will be flavorful for 6 months. Try it on cookies or use it to sweeten your coffee!

Citrus-flavored sugar: Mix together two cups of granulated sugar and 1/4 cup finely grated orange or lemon peel. Stir until well blended. Wait one week, then stir one more time before using.

Llwlyn Walker, from Lubbock, sent this wonderful sugar cookie recipe to us. Llwlyn has been a friend of my family for a long time. Her husband and my uncle, Dwayne West, played football together at Texas Tech. Years later her daughter Vickie and I were both Kappas at Tech. Isn't it neat when friendships not only continue, but grow! Llwlyn is currently the Women's Ministry Coordinator at First Baptist Church in Lubbock. She is a wonderful person with a sweet servant's heart. Thank you Llwlyn for sharing!

*K*aitlyn and I love to make these at Christmas. They have a great flavor and are crisp and moist at the same time. We like to cut out all kinds of Christmas shapes (not just gingerbread men). Then we decorate the cookies with white icing and red hots.

Our favorite White Icing is as follows:
½ cup shortening
½ cup butter
1 box powdered sugar
3 tablespoons milk
1 teaspoon vanilla

Cream shortening and butter. Gradually add powdered sugar alternating with milk. Stir in vanilla and beat until creamy.

Jolly Gingerbread

½	cup butter, softened
½	cup margarine, softened
1	cup sugar
1	egg
1	cup molasses
1	tablespoon vinegar
2	tablespoons water
5	cups all-purpose flour
2	teaspoons ground ginger
1½	teaspoons baking soda
1	teaspoon ground cinnamon
1	teaspoon ground cloves

Beat softened butter, margarine, and sugar together until fluffy. Add egg, molasses, vinegar, and water, beat well. To this, add baking soda and spices. Beat until well blended. Chill dough for 2 to 3 hours or until it is easy to handle. Roll out dough to ⅛ inch thickness and cut with shaped cookie cutters. In a 350° oven, bake for 5 to 8 minutes, or until done. Cool on a wire rack. When cool, decorate as desired.

Yield: 24 to 36 or more cookies depending on the size cookie cutters you use.

Note: Store in an air-tight container to keep them fresh.

Pineapple Cookies

½	cup shortening
½	cup brown sugar
½	cup granulated sugar
½	cup crushed pineapple, drained
½	cup pecans, broken
1	egg, well beaten
¼	teaspoon salt
¼	teaspoon baking soda (can be omitted for more cake-like cookies)
1	teaspoon baking powder
1	teaspoon vanilla
2	cups flour

Cream shortening with sugars. Add egg and pineapple. Mix thoroughly and add vanilla. Measure flour and sift with salt, baking soda, and baking powder. Add to first mixture plus the nuts. Mix thoroughly. Drop by teaspoonfuls onto a greased cookie sheet. Bake at 425° for approximately 10 minutes or until brown around the edges.

A favorite after school treat for Sue Haney and her sister. These delightful cookies have a cake-like texture and a nice twinge of pineapple flavor. They are also quick and easy to make. That is probably one of the reasons Sue's mother Winona Jones made them so often for the girls.

The kindly word that falls today may bear its fruit tomorrow.

Another favorite of the Haney family. Sue Haney shared that her mother Winona baked these fresh and served them warm to top off their Christmas morning breakfast for as long as she can remember! Sue's daughters Julie and Jill are now married, but they both still ask for these delightful cookies at holiday time. Christmas just would not be Christmas at the Haney home without Winona's Filled Cookies!

Winona's Filled Cookies

1	cup shortening
1	cup packed brown sugar
1	teaspoon orange rind
1	teaspoon lemon rind
½	teaspoon nutmeg
1	teaspoon vanilla
¼	teaspoon salt
1	egg
2¼	cups flour
1	teaspoon baking powder

Mix all ingredients. Divide dough into two parts. Roll each part into an approximate 2-inch diameter roll. Wrap in waxed paper or plastic wrap and chill for several hours. Cut into thin slices. Put filling on one slice of dough and cover with another. Press edges together and bake in a preheated 350° oven for 10 minutes or until golden brown.

Filling:

1	cup raisins
1	cup pecans, chopped
1	tablespoon flour
½	cup granulated sugar
½	teaspoon cinnamon
½	cup orange juice

Mix fruit, flour, and sugar together. Stir in remaining ingredients and let stand 10 minutes. Cook slowly until thick; stirring constantly. Let cool.

Note: Filling can be made ahead and refrigerated until ready to bake cookies.

Amaretto Brownies

1	cup sugar
½	cup vegetable oil
2	eggs
1	teaspoon vanilla extract
⅔	cup all-purpose flour
½	cup unsweetened cocoa powder
½	teaspoon baking powder
¾	cup coarsely chopped pecans
½	teaspoon salt

In a large mixing bowl, combine all ingredients. Beat with mixer on low speed for 2 minutes. Spread evenly in a 9x9-inch pan. Bake for 20 minutes in a preheated 350° oven. Cool completely. Spread with almond icing then drizzle with chocolate glaze.

Almond Icing:

1	(3-ounce) package cream cheese, softened
1	tablespoon butter or margarine, softened
3	cups powdered sugar
4-5	tablespoons milk
1	teaspoon almond extract

Combine all ingredients in mixing bowl and beat until smooth.

Chocolate Glaze:

1	(1-ounce) square semisweet chocolate
2	tablespoons butter

Melt chocolate and butter in microwave; stir until smooth.

I love the flavor of almond extract! And believe me this brownie is packed with flavor. From the rich chocolate brownie to the creamy almond flavored icing these brownies are scrumptious! They are also very pretty. For a unique presentation cut them into triangles or diamond shapes. MIx them on a platter with the Chocolate Almond Bars on page 188 and listen to your friends ooh and aah!

185

Cookies

*L*lwyn Walker sent us this wonderful rich gooey cookie recipe from her daughter Vickie Walker Moore. Vickie and I knew each other at Texas Tech. We were both Kappas. Vickie is married and lives in Hereford, Texas, and is the mother of three active teenagers.

*M*y cousin, Donna Bradley makes this wonderful treat. It is quick, easy, and delicious. It is a great treat for birthdays or other special occasions.

Gooey Turtle Bars

½	cup margarine, melted
1½	cups vanilla wafer crumbs
2	cups (12-ounces) semi-sweet chocolate chips
1	cup pecan pieces
1	(12-ounce) jar caramel topping

Combine melted margarine and crumbs. Place in a 9x13x2-inch pan. Sprinkle with chocolate chips and pecans. Microwave caramel for 1 to 1½ minutes on high, stirring once. Drizzle over chocolate chips and pecans. Bake in a 350° oven for 15 to 18 minutes. Cool in pan. Chill for 30 minutes before cutting into bars.

Donna's Giant M & M Cookie

Beat together one box yellow cake mix (the kind with pudding in it), 2 tablespoons water, 2 eggs, and ½ cup vegetable oil. Add one cup colored M&M's, ½ cup chocolate chips and 1 cup of nuts. Spread dough on a greased and floured 12-inch pizza pan.(Note: Donna takes out about a cup of dough and bakes it in another little pan because otherwise it always seems to overflow out of the pizza pan.) Bake at 325° for 20 minutes or until lightly brown. Let cool. Slice like pizza and enjoy!

Coconut Pecan Bars

½	pound butter
1	cup dark brown sugar
2	cups flour
4	eggs
2	cups light brown sugar
1½	cups grated coconut
2	tablespoons flour
1¾	cups pecans, chopped
¼	teaspoon salt
2	teaspoons vanilla
powdered sugar	

Cream butter and dark brown sugar. Gradually add 2 cups flour and mix well. Divide dough and press into two 9-inch square pans. Bake in a 350° oven for 20 minutes. Beat eggs until frothy and pale yellow. Gradually add light brown sugar and beat until thick. Toss coconut with 2 tablespoons flour and stir into sugar and egg mixture. Add pecans, salt, and vanilla to mixture; stir well. Spread over baked crust and bake an additional 20 minutes or until golden brown. When cool, dust with powdered sugar and cut into 1½-inch squares.

Yield: 6 dozen bars

Note: Don't be tempted to bake these in a large 9 x 13-inch pan. I tried that because I didn't have two 9-inch pans, but it was hard to get them done in the middle. This recipe is so good, the next time I made them, I made sure, I had two smaller pans.

When I featured this cookie at the Dallas Market, everyone pleaded for the recipe. Some people ordered this book simply to get this recipe! These are similar to pecan bars, but the coconut gives it an added flavor. Also do not substitute margarine for the butter. The butter adds to the rich flavor. In fact, they are so rich you can cut them into very small servings and still get rave reviews.

If you like Almond Joy candy bars, you will love this cookie! It uses a combination of those same wonderful ingredients- chocolate, coconut, and almonds. This is another scrumptious dessert from the good cooks at All Seasons.

The door to the human heart can only be opened from the inside.

Chocolate Almond Coconut Bars

1	cup flour
½	cup brown sugar
¼	cup butter, softened
1½	cups coconut
½	cup almonds, whole blanched
1	(14-ounce) can sweetened condensed milk, divided

Grease a 9-inch square, or 11x17-inch rectangular pan. Mix together flour, brown sugar, and butter. Press into bottom of pan. Combine coconut and ¾ cup of sweetened condensed milk; spread over crust. Place almonds evenly over coconut mixture. Bake in a 350° oven for 20 to 25 minutes.

Frosting:

1	cup semisweet chocolate chips
½	cup sweetened condensed milk
½	teaspoon vanilla

Over low heat, melt chocolate chips with sweetened condensed milk. Stir in vanilla. Spread over warm bars. Refrigerate 30 minutes then cut into bars.

Yield: 36 bars

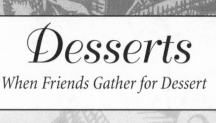

Desserts

When Friends Gather for Dessert

*And since I have no
gold to give,
And love alone
must make amends,
My only prayer is,
while I live-
God make me worthy
of my friends.*

Frank Dempster Sherman

*N*ot only is this easy to make and wonderfully delicious; it fills your home with an incredible aroma!

Helpful Hint: Invest in one of those neat gadgets that peels, cores, and slices the apples all at once. Even if you only use it to make this recipe and an occasional apple pie, it is worth the investment!

Susan's Apple Crisp

5	large Jonagold apples, peeled, cored, and sliced
1½	teaspoons cinnamon
½	teaspoon nutmeg
½	cup water
¾	cup all-purpose flour
1	stick of butter, chilled and sliced
½	cup granulated sugar
½	cup brown sugar, packed

Place the sliced apples in a large bowl. Sprinkle with cinnamon and nutmeg. Toss to coat. Spoon apples into a 9x13-inch (or larger) glass baking dish that has been sprayed with nonstick cooking spray. Pour ½ cup of water over apples. In a medium bowl, combine flour, butter, sugar, and brown sugar. Using a pastry blender or a fork, mix until mixture is crumbly. Spoon over apples. Bake at 400° for 40 to 45 minutes or until golden brown. Remove from oven and cool for 15 minutes. Serve with a scoop of vanilla ice cream.

Note: I really like to use Jonagold apples in this recipe. They are firm and are not too sweet. Jonagold apples are a cross between a Jonathan and Golden Delicious apple. They have red-streaked yellow skin. If Jonagold apples are not available, try any variety that is good for baking like a Jonathan, Golden Delicious, or Rome Beauty.

Pumpkin Crunch Dessert

3	eggs, slightly beaten
1	cup brown sugar
1	(15-ounce) can of pumpkin
1	(12-ounce) can evaporated milk
½	teaspoon salt
½	teaspoon nutmeg
½	teaspoon ground cloves
1	teaspoon cinnamon
1	(18.25-ounce) box yellow cake mix, dry
1	cup coarsely chopped pecans
1½	sticks of butter, melted
	whipped topping

Mix first 8 ingredients together until well blended and creamy. Pour into a greased 9x13-inch baking dish. Combine dry cake mix and chopped pecans. Sprinkle on top of pumpkin mixture. Drizzle melted butter on top. Bake in a 375° oven for 12 minutes. Reduce heat and cook at 325° for 30 minutes. Serve with a dollop of whipped cream or whipped topping.

My mom and her sister Jane had a cake similar to this at a tea room near Houston. It was so good that they described it to me, and we recreated the recipe. This is a great dessert to serve when the weather turns crisp and cool outside and autumn is on its way.

A soul friend is someone with whom we can share our greatest joys and deepest fears.

This cheesecake recipe was one of Fern Igo's legendary desserts. Martha Birdwell shared it with us and said, "I can hardly remember a special occasion with Fern that she didn't serve this cheesecake." Fern was an incredible cook and a wonderful person. She and Martha shared a special friendship. One that was tested and strengthened through time as they shared both abundant joys and deep sorrows. Everytime Martha makes one of Fern's recipes she and her family are filled with sweet memories!

Fern's Cheesecake

⅔	cup ziewback crumbs
3	(8-ounce) packages cream cheese,softened
4	egg whites
1	cup sugar
1	teaspoon vanilla

Add vanilla to cream cheese. Whip cream cheese until fluffy. Beat egg whites until frothy. Add sugar to egg whites slowly and beat until stiff. Fold cream cheese into egg whites. Butter an 8-inch spring form pan. Dust pan with ⅔ cup ziewback crumbs. Pour cream cheese mixture into pan and bake for 25 minutes in a 350° oven.

2nd layer:

2	cups sour cream
2	tablespoons sugar
½	teaspoon vanilla

Mix ingredients together and pour over top of cake. Add slivered almonds on top and bake at 475° for 5 minutes.

Yield: 8 servings

Mocha-Pecan Scones

2	cups flour
2	teaspoons baking powder
½	teaspoon baking soda
½	teaspoon salt
½	cup sugar, heaping
⅓	cup margarine, cold
½	cup buttermilk
1	large egg, lightly beaten
2-3	teaspoons instant espresso powder
½	cup chopped pecans
½	cup chocolate mini-chips

Preheat oven to 425°. Combine first 5 ingredients; cut in margarine. In a separate bowl, combine buttermilk, egg, and espresso powder; stir until powder is mostly dissolved. Add buttermilk mixture, pecans, and chocolate chips to dry ingredients; stir just until moist. Turn dough out onto floured surface and knead 5 times. Divide into ¼'s. Roll or pat each quarter into a circle. Cut into 8 wedges. Place wedges on a lightly greased or parchment lined baking sheet. Brush with milk and sprinkle heavily with sugar. Bake for 10 to 12 minutes or until very lightly browned.

Drizzle Topping: (optional)

½   cup mini-chocolate chips

Place chips in a heavy zip-top plastic bag and submerge bag in warm water until chips melt. Snip a tiny corner off bag and drizzle over warm scones.

Yield: 32 scones

*S*ue Ellen Bumpus *shared this delightful dessert! She took them to All Seasons several years ago. Now Sherry Brandt and Rosemary will not let her paint with them unless she brings these delicious scones! Sue Ellen is happy to oblige because she thinks the world of these two talented painters. Besides, food, friendship, and fun have been a part of All Seasons' success since it's beginning!*

This is the petite cheesecake recipe from my first cookbook, but the wonderful presentation idea comes from Kelly Sue Whitten of Plainview, Texas. When I was the speaker at Kelly Sue's study club luncheon, the ladies there prepared the entire menu out of my first cookbook, "Where Hearts Gather". Their beautiful presentation of these simple little cheesecakes turned an ordinary dessert into a gourmet delight!

Petite Cheesecakes with Praline Sauce

2	(8-ounce) packages cream cheese, softened
3/4	cup sugar
2	eggs
1	tablespoon lemon juice
1	teaspoon vanilla
24	vanilla wafers

Beat cream cheese, sugar, eggs, lemon juice, and vanilla until light and fluffy. Line muffin pans with paper baking cups. Place one vanilla wafer in each cup. Fill 2/3 full. Bake at 375° for 15 to 20 minutes. Cool.

To assemble: Chill individual dessert plates. Drizzle chilled plates with chocolate sauce and caramel ice cream sauce (Note: The best way to do this is to put each sauce in a plastic squeeze bottle). Take cheesecakes out of paper liners and place one on each dessert plate. Spoon warm praline sauce (recipe below) over each cheesecake. Serve immediately.

Praline Sauce

To make sauce: In a saucepan, combine 1 cup light corn syrup, 1/2 cup sugar, 1/3 cup butter, and 1 egg beaten. Stir until well mixed. Bring to a boil over medium-heat, stirring constantly. Boil 2 minutes without stirring. Remove from heat and add 1 tablespoon vanilla and 1 cup coarsely chopped pecans. Serve warm over cheesecakes.

Jane's Scrumptious Cherry-Raspberry Topping

1	**(16-ounce) can cherry pie filling**
1	**package frozen raspberries**
½-1	**cup sugar**

Place frozen raspberries in a bowl with ½ cup of sugar. Set aside and let thaw. When berries are thawed, microwave for 2 minutes, stirring several times until sugar dissolves. Add more sugar if you would like mixture sweeter. Stir in cherry pie filling. Chill for several hours or overnight. Serve over angel food cake with a dollop of whipped topping.

Note: Jane serves this over an Angel Food Cake, but I think it would be wonderful over any pound cake. Try it over Herbert's Pound Cake on page 141, our Chocolate Sour Cream Pound Cake on page 142, or even Pam's Butter Cake on page 149.

*J*ane Bryant often serves this wonderful dessert. I had the pleasure of enjoying it recently, and it is delicious! The sauce makes a dessert beautiful because of its pretty red color. The other great thing is, it is sooo easy! But don't tell your guests how simple it is to make; just let them say "This is incredible!"

God gives us our relatives, but thank heavens we can choose our friends!

My daughter, Kaitlyn and I were baking desserts for the Mother-Daughter luncheon at her school. I wanted to make the petite praline cheese-cakes, but she wanted something chocolate, so we created this recipe. It was such a hit at the luncheon, every-one wanted the recipe!

*Some people come
into our lives
and quickly go,
Some stay
awhile
and leave
footprints
on our hearts,
and we are
never the same.*

Flavia Weeden

Kaitlyn's Chocolate Chip Cheesecakes

2	(8-ounce) packages cream cheese, softened
¾	cup sugar
2	eggs
1	tablespoon lemon juice
1	teaspoon vanilla
1	cup mini semi-sweet chocolate chips
24	chocolate vanilla wafers

Beat cream cheese, sugar, eggs, lemon juice, and vanilla until light and fluffy. Add the mini chocolate chips and mix well. Line muffin pans with paper liners. Put one chocolate vanilla wafer in each. (Note: If you cannot find the chocolate wafers, use regular vanilla wafers.) Fill cups ⅔ full. Bake at 375° for 15 to 20 minutes or until lightly brown around the edges. Cool. In a heavy zip-top freezer bag, or any microwave-safe bag, melt 1 cup of semi-sweet chocolate chips in the microwave on medium power. Once chips are melted, snip a tiny hole in one corner of the bag. Drizzle chocolate over the cheesecakes. Chill and enjoy!

Yield: 24 individual cheesecakes

Caramel Chocolate Delight

1	large package Oreo cookies, crushed
¼	cup butter or margarine, melted
½	gallon vanilla ice cream, softened
6	Heath candy bars, crushed
1	(12-ounce) jar caramel ice cream topping
1	(8-ounce) frozen whipped topping, thawed

Combine crushed cookies and melted butter. Press into the bottom of a 9x13-inch baking dish. Scoop softened ice cream onto cookie crumb crust and smooth evenly over crust. Sprinkle crushed candy bars over ice cream then cover with caramel topping. Spread whipped topping and sprinkle with chopped pecans. Freeze and cut into squares when ready to serve.

Yield: 10-12 servings

This easy dessert is yummy! It combines several of my favorite flavors including caramel and chocolate. It is also a good dessert to prepare ahead of time.

Quick Tip: Set the jar of caramel in a bowl of hot water while you prepare crust or remove the lid and microwave on medium just until caramel is warm and pours easily.

*M*y family has enjoyed this recipe since I was a kid! I have traced its origin to an old church cookbook. The cookbook is from Riverside Methodist Church in Fort Worth, Texas. Beside the recipe is the name Mary Lou Lewis, a dear sweet friend of my family!

Note: This is a great dessert to feed a large group of hungry teenagers! It is easy to make and can be prepared several days ahead of time.

Fudge Stuff

1½	cups vanilla wafer crumbs
¼	cup melted butter or margarine
1	stick of butter
1	(2-ounce) package unsweetened chocolate
3	eggs, separated
2	cups powdered sugar
1	dash of salt
½	gallon vanilla ice cream, softened

Combine vanilla wafer crumbs and ¼ cup of melted butter. Press crumb mixture in the bottom of a 9x13-inch baking dish to form the crust. In a medium sauce pan, melt chocolate with 1 stick of butter over low heat. Stir in egg yolks, powdered sugar, and salt. Remove from burner. Beat egg whites and fold into chocolate mixture. Alternately layer softened ice cream and chocolate mixture over crumb crust. Top with additional vanilla wafer crumbs. Freeze. Cut into squares when ready to serve.

Yield: 18 servings

Note: If you are serving teenagers you better plan for seconds or large helpings to begin with!

Wonderful Ice Cream

6	eggs, separated
3	cups sugar
4	½ pints of whipping cream
2	teaspoons vanilla
2	teaspoons lemon extract
2	tablespoons flour

pinch of salt
Milk

Beat egg whites well, then add 1½ cups of sugar and beat for about 15 minutes. Combine 1½ cups sugar, flour and salt. Beat egg yolks then add sugar mixture. Continue to beat for 15 minutes. Combine egg white and egg yolk mixtures and beat for 30 minutes. Add whipping cream, vanilla and lemon flavoring; mix well. Pour into freezer and finish filling with milk. Freeze according to your freezers instructions.

Yield: 1-gallon

Note: Sandy said the secret to this recipe is in the beating. Do not rush it! She suggests that you just leave your mixer going, set a timer and do something else for the next 30 minutes! The results are worth it!

*T*his recipe has been in Sandy Lindeman's family for over 30 years! Sandy first tasted it at a baby shower given for her when she was pregnant with her daughter. Sandy said, "It was absolutely the best ice cream I had ever eaten!" It has become a family favorite and a <u>must</u> for birthday celebrations!

A friend understands what you are trying to say... even when your thoughts aren't fitting into words.

199

aurine Hill served this incredible ice cream one summer evening. If you like cheesecake like I do, you will LOVE this ice cream!!! It is incredibly rich so a small serving is very satisfying. It's especially good with sliced fresh summer peaches or strawberries. Maurine and I have been friends for many years. Our daughters go to the same school, and our families attend the same church. Maurine is also a great cook too. If you're looking for a dessert that will make your guests say "Wow!" this is the dessert!

Maurine's Cheesecake Ice Cream

5	egg yolks
2¼	cups sugar
1½	pints half-and-half
3	(8-ounce) packages of cream cheese
3	tablespoons lemon juice
3	teaspoons vanilla
1½	pints plain yogurt

Combine egg yolks and ¾ cup sugar in a 4 cup glass dish. Whisk in half-and-half. Microwave on high 5 to 5½ minutes, whisking midway through cooking. Refrigerate. Place cream cheese in glass mixing bowl and microwave on 50% power for 3 to 3½ minutes. Beat in remaining 1½ cups sugar, lemon juice, and vanilla. Add yogurt and chilled egg mixture. Beat until smooth. Place in ice cream freezer and freeze.

Yield: 4-quarts

Do not be overly concerned with the interior of your home, because it's the inside of your heart that guests will remember.

Anne Platz

Index

A

All Seasons' Chicken Salad 90
All Seasons' Pasta Salad 89
Almond Crunch Cookies 170
Almond Icing 185
Amaretto Brownies 185
Ambrosia Salad 95

APPETIZERS *(See also Dips and Spreads)*
Marinated Appetizer 16
Marlena's Spicy Do-Dads 19
Orange Glazed Pecans 20
Parmesan Glazed Walnuts 19
Stuffed Cherry Tomatoes 15
Sweet & Spicy Pecans 18
Texas Spiced Pecans 12
Texas Trail Mix 18
Turkey Club Rollups 13

APPLES AND APPLE JUICE
Apple Orchard Punch 25
Green Apple Salad 93
Rosemary's Apple
Candy Pie 153
Susan's Apple Crisp 190
Applesauce Cake 152
Applesauce Spiced Muffins 45

ARTICHOKES

Baked Cheese Dip in
Sourdough Bread 17
Fresh Garden Salad 82
Marinated Appetizer 16
Aunt Elsie's Oatmeal Cookies 178

AVOCADOES

Black-Eyed Pea Dip 9
Cucumber-Avocado Dip 14
Guacamole 10
Mandarin Orange Salad 86

B

Bacon Tomato Dip 14
Baked Cheese Dip in
Sourdough Bread 17
Baked Potato Soup 51

BANANAS

Aunt Donna's Blueberry
Banana Pie 156
Daisy's Banana Nut Bread 66
Barbeque Chicken Pizza 112

BEANS AND PEAS

Black Bean and Rice
Layered Casserole 118
Black-Eyed Pea Dip 9

Index

Cowboy Stew 54

French Bean Casserole 125

Fresh Green Beans 71

Paula's Baked Beans 124

Santa Fe Soup 56

Southwest Roast 115

Upside-Down Chalupa 120

White Chicken Chili 55

BEEF

Cowboy Stew 54

Green Chile Beef Quiche 116

Pepper Crusted Roast Beef 114

Roast Gravy 114

Santa Fe Soup 56

Southwest Roast 115

Taco Bake 117

BEVERAGES

Apple Orchard Punch 25

Cafe Mexican 33

Caramel Chocolate Mocha 33

Cherry Cranberry Cooler 26

Fruit Tea 23

Hot Apple Punch 31

Lemon Almond Tea 24

Making an Ice Ring 29

Pam's Tea 22

Paradise Punch 27

Pretty Party Punch 30

Spiced Apple Punch 31

Spiced Mocha Mix 34

Summer Sun Tea 23

The Perfect Cup of Coffee 32

Viennese Spiced Coffee 34

Wedding Punch 28

BLUEBERRIES

Aunt Donna's Blueberry
Banana Pie 156

Blueberry Salad 99

Summer Berry Pie 164

BREADS AND MUFFINS

Applesauce Spiced Muffins 45

Bread Machine
Pizza Dough 113

Cheese Garlic Biscuits 58

Cream Cheese Biscuits 60

Daisy's Banana Nut Bread 66

Grammy's Homemade
Cinnamon Rolls 76

Herb Garden Bread 63

Homemade Pimento Cheese 62

Hot Ham & Cheese
Sandwiches 62

Llwlyn's Cornbread 57

Mary's Strawberry Bread 64

Mom's Homemade Rolls 75

Pecan Pie Muffins 46

Sausage Cheese Muffins 44

Savory Cheese Loaf.................... 61

Savory Cream Corn Biscuits 58

Sesame Bread 59

Sweet Potato Bread 65

BREAKFAST & BRUNCH *(See also Breads)*

Applesauce Spiced Muffins 45

Ham and Green Chile
    Breakfast Casserole 36

Homemade Syrup 48

Logan's Favorite
    Cinnamon Cake 43

Maple Cream Cheese
    Frosting 41

Oatmeal Spice Coffeecake 40

Orange Almond
    French Toast 47

Pecan Pie Muffins 46

Poppy Seed Cake 38

Raspberry Cream
    Cheese Coffee Cake 39

Sausage Cheese Muffins 44

Sausage Parmesan
    Breakfast Bake 37

Sour Cream Coffee Cake 42

Breast of Chicken
    Magnificent 102

BROCCOLI

Broccoli Salad 88

Buffalo Chip Cookies 171

Butter Cookies 179

Butter Crunch Crust 156

Buttermilk Pie 158

Butterscotch Cookies 175

C

CABBAGE

Chinese Cabbage Salad 92

Cafe Mexican 33

Cakes *(See Desserts)*

Calico Corn Casserole 74

Canadian Cheese Soup 52

Caramel Chocolate Chip
    Ice Cream Pie 168

Caramel Chocolate Delight 197

Caramel Chocolate Mocha 33

Caramel Coconut Pie 155

Caramelized Onions 112

CARROTS

Carrot Cake 145

Carrot Souffle 122

Index

Squash & Carrot Julienne 134

CASSEROLES

Black Bean and Rice
Layered Casserole 118

Calico Corn Casserole 74

Corn Casserole 122

Crunchy Chicken Salad
Casserole 108

Edith's "No-Keno"
Chicken Casserole 107

French Bean Casserole 125

Ham and Green Chile
Breakfast Casserole 36

Mexican Festival Corn
and Rice Casserole 136

Mother's Cornbread
Dressing 135

Mrs. Adams Corn Casserole 123

Party Potato Casserole 128

Poppy Seed Chicken
and Rice Casserole 106

Sue's Layered Potato
Casserole 129

Summer Vegetable
Casserole 134

CHEESE

All Seasons' Pasta Salad 89

Baked Cheese Dip in
Sourdough Bread 17

Baked Potato Soup 51

Barbeque Chicken Pizza 112

Black Bean and Rice
Layered Casserole 118

Calico Corn Casserole 74

Canadian Cheese Soup 52

Cheese Garlic Biscuits 58

Edith's "No-Keno"
Chicken Casserole 107

French Bean Casserole 125

Green Chile Beef Quiche 116

Haughton Girls Party Salad 84

Homemade Macaroni
& Cheese 73

Homemade Pimento Cheese 62

Hot Ham & Cheese
Sandwiches 62

Hot Southwest Corn Dip 12

Mexican Festival Corn
and Rice Casserole 136

Old-Fashion
Chicken Spaghetti 72

Rice Con Queso 137

Sausage Cheese Muffins 44

Sausage Parmesan
Breakfast Bake 37

Savory Cheese Loaf 61

Sin Spuds 126

Southwestern Cheese Dip 8

Sue's Layered Potato
Casserole 129

Taco Bake 117

Texas Rice 138

Zesty Chicken Spaghetti 105

Chicken *(See Poultry)*

CHERRIES

Cherry Cranberry Cooler 26

French Cherry Pie 163

Jane's Scrumptious Cherry-
Raspberry Topping 195

Chinese Cabbage Salad 92

CHOCOLATE *(See also Desserts)*

Amaretto Brownies 185

Buffalo Chip Cookies 171

Caramel Chocolate Chip
Ice Cream Pie 168

Caramel Chocolate Delight 197

Caramel Chocolate Mocha 33

Chocolate Almond
Coconut Bars 188

Chocolate Chess Pie 158

Chocolate Chip Pound Cake 78

Chocolate Dipped
Strawberries 146

Chocolate Dream Cake 150

Chocolate Dream Frosting 151

Chocolate Glaze 147, 185

Chocolate Silk Pie 157

Chocolate Sour Cream
Pound Cake 142

Fudge Stuff 198

Gooey Turtle Bars 186

Hidden Kisses 173

Kaitlyn's Chocolate
Chip Cheesecakes 196

Mocha-Pecan Scones 193

Peanut Butter Surprise 176

Reba's Chocolate Pie 165

Spiced Mocha Mix 34

COCONUT

Ambrosia Salad 95

Caramel Coconut Pie 155

Chocolate Almond
Coconut Bars 188

Coconut Pecan Bars 187

Coconut Pineapple Pie 159

Earthquake Cake 148

Jane's Coconut Caramel Pie 154

Oatmeal Crisps 177

Reba's Coconut Pie 166

Vanilla Wafer Cake 147

CONDIMENTS

Grilled Chicken with Corn and
Roasted Pepper Relish 109

Pico de Gallo 111

Index

Cookies *(See Desserts)*

CORN

Calico Corn Casserole 74

Corn Casserole 122

Cowboy Stew 54

Grilled Chicken with
Corn and Roasted
Pepper Relish 109

Hot Southwest Corn Dip 12

Mexican Festival Corn
and Rice Casserole 136

Mrs. Adams Corn Casserole 123

Santa Fe Soup 56

Savory Cream Corn Biscuits 58

White Chicken Chili 55

Zucchini Corn Medley 133

CRANBERRIES

Cranberry Salad 98

Cream Cheese Biscuits 60

Cream Cheese Icing 146

Cream Cheese Tomato Soup 53

Cream Gravy 70

Crunchy Chicken
Salad Casserole 108

CUCUMBERS

Cucumber-Avocado Dip 14

D

Daisy's Banada Nut Bread 66

Dell's Grilled Chicken Fajitas 110

DESSERTS *(See also Chocolate)*

Cake Frostings, Icings and
Toppings

Chocolate Dream
Frosting 151

Chocolate Glaze 147

Cream Cheese Icing 146

Jane's Scrumptious Cherry-
Raspberry Topping 195

Maple Cream
Cheese Frosting 41

Our Favorite White Icing 182

Praline Sauce 194

Cakes

Applesauce Cake 152

Carrot Cake 145

Chocolate Chip
Pound Cake 78

Chocolate Dream Cake 150

Chocolate Sour Cream
Pound Cake 142

Earthquake Cake 148

Fresh Pear Cake 144

Herbert's Pound Cake 141

Lemon Pound Cake 140

Logan's Favorite
Cinnamon Cake 43

Nona's Best Buttermilk
Pound Cake 77

Oatmeal Cake 143

Oatmeal Spice Coffeecake 40

Pam's Butter Cake 149

Poppy Seed Cake 38

Raspberry Cream
Cheese Coffee Cake 39

Sour Cream Coffee Cake 42

Vanilla Wafer Cake 147

Cookies and Bars

Almond Crunch Cookies 170

Almond Icing 185

Amaretto Brownies 185

Aunt Elsie's Oatmeal
Cookies 178

Buffalo Chip Cookies 171

Butter Cookies 179

Butterscotch Cookies 175

Chocolate Almond
Coconut Bars 188

Chocolate Glaze 185

Coconut Pecan Bars 187

Donna's Giant
M & M Cookie 186

Gooey Turtle Bars 186

Hidden Kisses 173

Jolly Gingerbread 182

Karen's Old Fashion
Rolled Sugar Cookies 174

Melting Moments 172

Oatmeal Crisps 177

Our Favorite White Icing 182

Peanut Butter Surprise 176

Pineapple Cookies 183

Stenciled Gingerbread
Hearts 180

Sugar Cookies 181

Winona's Filled Cookies 184

Ice Cream

Maurine's Cheesecake
Ice Cream 200

Wonderful Ice Cream 199

Pies

Aunt Donna's Blueberry
Banana Pie 156

Butter Crunch Crust 156

Buttermilk Pie 158

Caramel Chocolate Chip
Ice Cream Pie 168

Caramel Coconut Pie 155

Chocolate Chess Pie 158

Chocolate Silk Pie 157

Coconut Pineapple Pie 159

French Cherry Pie 163

Index

Graham Cracker Crust 167

Jane's Coconut
Caramel Pie 154

Mystic Pie 160

Never Fail Meringue............. 165

Peanut Butter Silk Pie 161

Pink Surprise
Lemonade Pie 167

Reba's Chocolate Pie 165

Reba's Coconut Pie 166

Rosemary's Apple
Candy Pie.......................... 153

Summer Berry Pie 164

Texas Pecan Pie 162

Puddings and Desserts

Caramel Chocolate
Delight 197

Chocolate Dipped
Strawberries 146

Fern's Cheesecake................. 192

Fudge Stuff 198

Jane's Scrumptious
Cherry-Raspberry
Topping 195

Kaitlyn's Chocolate
Chip Cheesecakes 196

Mocha-Pecan Scones 193

Petite Cheesecakes
with Praline Sauce 194

Pumpkin Crunch Dessert 191

Susan's Apple Crisp 190

DIPS AND SPREADS

Bacon Tomato Dip 14

Baked Cheese Dip
in Sourdough Bread 17

Black-Eyed Pea Dip 9

Cucumber-Avocado Dip 14

Guacamole 10

Hot Southwest Corn Dip 12

Pico de Gallo 111

Southwestern Cheese Dip 8

Stacey's Salsa 11

Donna's Giant M & M Cookie 186

E

Earthquake Cake 148

Edith's "No-Keno"
Chicken Casserole 107

F

Fern's Cheesecake 192

Fiesta Potatoes 127

French Bean Casserole 125

French Cherry Pie 163

Fresh Garden Salad 82

Fresh Green Beans 71

Fresh Pear Cake 144

FRUIT *(See also individual listings)*
  Fruit Basket Salad 96
  Fruit Tea 23
Fudge Stuff 198

G

Gooey Turtle Bars 186
Graham Cracker Crust 167
Grammy's Homemade
    Cinnamon Rolls 76
Grandmother's Baked Squash 71

GRAPES
  All Seasons' Chicken Salad 90

GRAVIES
  Cream Gravy 70
  Roast Gravy 114
  Sour Cream Gravy 119
Green Apple Salad 93
Green Chile Beef Quiche 116

GRILLING RECIPES
  Dell's Grilled Chicken Fajitas 110
  Grilled Chicken with Corn and
      Roasted Pepper Relish 109
  Grilled Peppers and Onions 111

Guacamole 10

H

Ham and Green Chile
    Breakfast Casserole 36
Haughton Girls Party Salad 84
Herb Garden Bread 63
Herbert's Pound Cake 141
Hidden Kisses 173
Homemade Chicken
    Noodle Soup 50
Homemade Macaroni
    & Cheese 73
Homemade Mashed Potatoes 70
Homemade Pimento Cheese 62
Homemade Syrup 48
Hot Apple Punch 31
Hot Ham & Cheese
    Sandwiches 62
Hot Southwest Corn Dip 12

J

Jane's Coconut Caramel Pie 154
Jane's Scrumptious
    Cherry-Raspberry Topping 195
Jolly Gingerbread 182
Juli's Favorite Spinach Salad 83

Index

K

Kaitlyn's Chocolate
Chip Cheesecakes 196

Karen's Old Fashion
Rolled Sugar Cookies 174

L

Lemon Almond Tea 24

Lemon Pound Cake 140

LEMONS

Lemon Almond Tea 24

Llwlyn's Cornbread 57

Logan's Favorite
Cinnamon Cake 43

M

Making an Ice Ring 29

Mandarin Orange Salad 86

Maple Cream Cheese Frosting 41

Marinated Appetizer 16

Marlena's Spicy Do-Dads 19

Mary's Strawberry Bread 64

Maurine's Cheesecake
Ice Cream 200

Melting Moments 172

Mexican Chicken Salad 91

Mexican Festival Corn
and Rice Casserole 136

Mocha-Pecan Scones 193

Mom's Homemade Rolls 75

Mother's Cornbread Dressing 135

Mrs. Adams Corn Casserole 123

Murfreesboro Fried Chicken 69

MUSHROOMS

Breast of Chicken
Magnificent 102

Juli's Favorite Spinach Salad 83

Marinated Appetizer 16

Sour Cream Gravy 119

Mystic Pie 160

N

Never Fail Meringue 165

Nona's Best Buttermilk
Pound Cake 77

NUTS

Almond Crunch Cookies 170

Applesauce Spiced Muffins 45

Buffalo Chip Cookies 171

Butterscotch Cookies 175

Chocolate Almond
Coconut Bars 188

Coconut Pecan Bars 187

Daisy's Banana Nut Bread 66

Hidden Kisses 173

Marlena's Spicy Do-Dads 19

Mocha-Pecan Scones 193

Orange Almond
   French Toast 47

Orange Glazed Pecans 20

Parmesan Glazed Walnuts 19

Pecan Chicken 103

Pecan Pie Muffins 46

Pistachio Salad 100

Spring Strawberry Salad 94

Sweet & Spicy Pecans 18

Texas Pecan Pie 162

Texas Spiced Pecans 12

Texas Trail Mix 18

O

Oatmeal Cake 143

Oatmeal Crisps 177

Oatmeal Spice Coffeecake 40

Old-Fashion
   Chicken Spaghetti 72

OLIVES
   Marinated Appetizer 16

ONIONS
   Caramelized Onions 112

   Grilled Peppers and Onions 111

Orange Glazed Pecans 20

ORANGES
   All Seasons' Chicken Salad 90

   Mandarin Orange Salad 86

   Orange Almond
      French Toast 47

Our Favorite White Icing 182

P

Pam's Butter Cake 149

Pam's Tea 22

Paradise Punch 27

Parker Potatoes 130

Parmesan Glazed Walnuts 19

Party Potato Casserole 128

PASTA
   All Seasons' Pasta Salad 89

   Chicken Pasta Salad 87

   Homemade Macaroni
      & Cheese 73

   Old-Fashion
      Chicken Spaghetti 72

   Taco Bake 117

   Zesty Chicken Spaghetti 105

Paula's Baked Beans 124

Peach Jello 100

Peanut Butter Silk Pie 161

Peanut Butter Surprise 176

Index

Pear Cake, Fresh 144

Pecan Chicken 103

Pecan Pie Muffins 46

Pepper Crusted Roast Beef.......... 114

PEPPERS

Green Chile Beef Quiche 116

Grilled Chicken with Corn and
    Roasted Pepper Relish 109

Grilled Peppers
    and Onions 111

Ham and Green Chile
    Breakfast Casserole 36

Hot Southwest Corn Dip 12

Pico de Gallo 111

Southwestern Cheese Dip 8

Stacey's Salsa 11

White Chicken Chili 55

Petite Cheesecakes
    with Praline Sauce 194

Pico de Gallo 111

Pies *(See Desserts)*

PINEAPPLE

Ambrosia Salad 95

Coconut Pineapple Pie 159

Cranberry Salad 98

Peach Jello 100

Pineapple Cookies 183

Pink Surprise Lemonade Pie 167

Pistachio Salad 100

PIZZAS

Barbeque Chicken Pizza 112

Bread Machine
    Pizza Dough 113

Poppy Seed Cake 38

Poppy Seed Chicken
    and Rice Casserole 106

Poppy Seed Dressing 93

PORK

All Seasons' Pasta Salad 89

Bacon Tomato Dip 14

Baked Potato Soup 51

Black Bean and Rice
    Layered Casserole 118

Broccoli Salad 88

Ham and Green Chile
    Breakfast Casserole 36

Haughton Girls Party Salad 84

Hot Ham & Cheese
    Sandwiches 62

Roast Pork with
    Sour Cream Gravy 119

Sausage Cheese Muffins 44

Sausage Parmesan
    Breakfast Bake 37

Savory Cheese Loaf..................... 61

Sin Spuds 126

Stuffed Cherry Tomatoes 15

Sue's Layered Potato
Casserole 129

Upside-Down Chalupa 120

POTATOES

Baked Potato Soup 51

Cowboy Stew 54

Fiesta Potatoes 127

Homemade Mashed
Potatoes 70

Parker Potatoes 130

Party Potato Casserole 128

Sin Spuds 126

Sue's Layered Potato
Casserole 129

POULTRY

Chicken

All Seasons' Chicken Salad 90

Barbeque Chicken Pizza 112

Breast of Chicken
Magnificent 102

Chicken a la King 104

Chicken Pasta Salad 87

Crunchy Chicken
Salad Casserole 108

Dell's Grilled
Chicken Fajitas 110

Edith's "No-Keno"
Chicken Casserole 107

Grilled Chicken with
Corn and Roasted
Pepper Relish 109

Homemade Chicken
Noodle Soup 50

Mexican Chicken Salad 91

Murfreesboro
Fried Chicken 69

Old-Fashion
Chicken Spaghetti 72

Pecan Chicken 103

Poppy Seed Chicken
and Rice Casserole 106

White Chicken Chili 55

Zesty Chicken Spaghetti 105

Turkey

Turkey Club Rollups 13

Pretty Party Punch 30

PUMPKIN

Pumpkin Crunch Dessert 191

Q

QUICHE

Green Chile Beef Quiche 116

Index

R

RASPBERRIES

Jane's Scrumptious Cherry-
Raspberry Topping 195

Raspberry Cream Cheese
Coffee Cake 39

Summer Berry Pie 164

Reba's Chocolate Pie 165

Reba's Coconut Pie 166

RICE

Black Bean and Rice
Layered Casserole 118

Calico Corn Casserole 74

Crunchy Chicken Salad
Casserole 108

Mexican Festival Corn
and Rice Casserole 136

Poppy Seed Chicken
and Rice Casserole 106

Rice Con Queso 137

Spanish Rice 137

Texas Rice 138

Rice Con Queso 137

Roast Gravy 114

Roast Pork with
Sour Cream Gravy 119

Rosemary's Apple Candy Pie 153

S

SALAD DRESSINGS

Poppy Seed Dressing 93

SALADS

All Seasons' Chicken Salad 90

All Seasons' Pasta Salad 89

Ambrosia Salad 95

Blueberry Salad 99

Broccoli Salad 88

Chicken Pasta Salad 87

Chinese Cabbage Salad 92

Cranberry Salad 98

Fresh Garden Salad 82

Fruit Basket Salad 96

Green Apple Salad 93

Haughton Girls Party Salad 84

Juli's Favorite Spinach Salad 83

Mandarin Orange Salad 86

Mexican Chicken Salad 91

Peach Jello 100

Pistachio Salad 100

Spicy Applesauce Salad 98

Spring Strawberry Salad 94

Zucchini Salad 85

Sandwiches, Hot Ham & Cheese 62

Santa Fe Soup 56

Sausage Cheese Muffins 44

Sausage Parmesan
   Breakfast Bake 37

Savory Cheese Loaf 61

Savory Cream Corn Biscuits 58

Sesame Bread 59

Sin Spuds 126

SOUPS AND STEWS

   Baked Potato Soup 51

   Canadian Cheese Soup 52

   Cowboy Stew 54

   Cream Cheese Tomato Soup 53

   Homemade Chicken
      Noodle Soup 50

   Santa Fe Soup 56

   White Chicken Chili 55

Sour Cream Coffee Cake 42

Sour Cream Gravy 119

Southwest Roast 115

Southwestern Cheese Dip 8

Spanish Rice 137

Spiced Apple Punch 31

Spiced Mocha Mix 34

Spicy Applesauce Salad 98

SPINACH

   Haughton Girls Party Salad 84

   Juli's Favorite Spinach Salad 83

SQUASH *(See also Zucchini)*

   Grandmother's
      Baked Squash 71

   Squash & Carrot Julienne 134

   Squash Olé 131

   Summer Vegetable
      Casserole 134

Stacey's Salsa 11

Stenciled Gingerbread Hearts 180

STRAWBERRIES

   Chocolate Dipped
      Strawberries 146

   Mary's Strawberry Bread 64

   Spring Strawberry Salad 94

   Summer Berry Pie 164

Stuffed Cherry Tomatoes 15

Sue's Layered
   Potato Casserole 129

Sugar Cookies 181

Summer Berry Pie 164

Summer Sun Tea 23

Summer Vegetable Casserole 134

Susan's Apple Crisp 190

Sweet & Spicy Pecans 18

Sweet Potato Bread 65

T

Taco Bake 117

Index

Tejas Tomatoes 132

Texas Pecan Pie 162

Texas Rice 138

Texas Spiced Pecans 12

Texas Trail Mix 18

The Perfect Cup of Coffee 32

TOMATOES

All Seasons' Pasta Salad 89

Bacon Tomato Dip 14

Black-Eyed Pea Dip 9

Cream Cheese Tomato Soup 53

Pico de Gallo 111

Santa Fe Soup 56

Stacey's Salsa 11

Stuffed Cherry Tomatoes 15

Summer Vegetable
Casserole 134

Tejas Tomatoes 132

Turkey Club Rollups 13

U

Upside-Down Chalupa 120

V

Vanilla Wafer Cake 147

VEGETABLES *(See also individual listings)*

Fresh Garden Salad 82

Summer Vegetable
Casserole 134

Viennese Spiced Coffee 34

W

Wedding Punch 28

White Chicken Chili 55

Winona's Filled Cookies 184

Wonderful Ice Cream 199

Z

Zesty Chicken Spaghetti 105

ZUCCHINI *(See also Squash)*

Squash & Carrot Julienne 134

Zucchini Corn Medley 133

Zucchini Salad 85

Notes

Notes & Favorite Recipes

Calling all Cooks

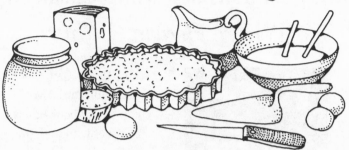

Do you have a special recipe that has a heartwarming story or memory?

Would you like to share?

We would love to hear from you!

We are especially looking for recipes that have been handed down from your mother, grandmother or great grandmother. Recipes like your mom's best pie or your grand mother's special recipe for chicken and dumplings. Please include their names, information about them, and why the recipe is special to your family. We also need your name and address, because if we use your recipe, you will receive a free copy of the cookbook in which your recipe appears!

Send your recipes and stories to:
Special Delivery Publications
5109-82nd, Suite 7, #204
Lubbock, Texas 79424
or e-mail us at: cookbooks@poka.com

For more great recipes and entertaining ideas....
Order our other best selling cookbooks!

Where Hearts Gather

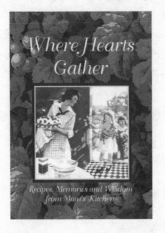

Where Hearts Gather is a
beautiful, hard cover,
comb bound book. It has
224 pages with over 200
tried and true recipes.

$16.95 plus $3.00 S&H

Filled with over 200 recipes for family favorites! This is the best of the best from four generations. A true treasure of delicious, easy to prepare, "real food". You will find recipes for delights like: Grammy's Cinnamon Rolls, Lemon Chess Pie, and Fresh Apple Cake. Or tempt your family with delicious main courses like Green Chili Beef Stew, Cheesy Chicken Vegetable Soup, or comforting standards like Mom's Meat Loaf.

Move Over Martha!

Move Over Martha
has a soft cover and
is comb bound.
There are 80 pages
full of tips, ideas, and
recipes.

$9.95 plus $3.00 S&H

Tired of the "Martha" standard of entertaining? Move Over Martha has the answer! Inside you will find the ABC's of hospitality and simple entertaining ideas for the way we live. Included are over 100 helpful hints, plus 30 new recipes and 10 classic favorites. Rediscover the simple art of hospitality from the heart. Order your copy today.

Order Form

Special Delivery Publications
5109-82nd, Suite 7, #204   Lubbock, TX 79424

Please send _____ copies of When Friends Gather @ $16.95 ea._____
Please send _____ copies of Move Over Martha   @ $10.95 ea. _____
Please send _____ copies of Where Hearts Gather @ $16.95 ea. _____

Postage and Handling per book ----------------------$ 3.00 ea. _____

Subtotal _____

Texas residents add 6.25 % sales tax _____

Total _____

Name:_____ Address: _____

City: _____ State: _____ Zip: _____

Phone number: (_____) _____

Make checks payable to: Special Delivery Publications
To place an order with your Visa, MasterCard
or American Express, call **800-533-8983**
or visit us on line @ **www.whereheartsgather.com**

Special Delivery Publications
5109-82nd, Suite 7, #204   Lubbock, TX 79424

Please send _____ copies of When Friends Gather @ $16.95 ea._____
Please send _____ copies of Move Over Martha   @ $10.95 ea. _____
Please send _____ copies of Where Hearts Gather @ $16.95 ea. _____

Postage and Handling per book ----------------------$ 3.00 ea. _____

Subtotal _____

Texas residents add 6.25 % sales tax _____

Total _____

Name:_____ Address: _____

City: _____ State: _____ Zip: _____

Phone number: (_____) _____

Make checks payable to: Special Delivery Publications
To place an order with your Visa, MasterCard
or American Express, call **800-533-8983**
or visit us on line @ **www.whereheartsgather.com**

Please list names and addresses of your favorite stores where you would like to see cookbooks from Special Delivery Publications sold.

_____

_____

_____

_____

_____

_____

_____

_____

_____

· ·

Please list names and addresses of your favorite stores where you would like to see cookbooks from Special Delivery Publications sold.

_____

_____

_____

_____

_____

_____

_____

Order Form

Special Delivery Publications
5109-82nd, Suite 7, #204   Lubbock, TX 79424

Please send _____ copies of When Friends Gather @ $16.95 ea._____
Please send _____ copies of Move Over Martha   @ $10.95 ea. _____
Please send _____ copies of Where Hearts Gather @ $16.95 ea. _____

Postage and Handling per book ----------------------$ 3.00 ea. _____
Subtotal _____
Texas residents add 6.25 % sales tax _____
Total _____
Name:_____ Address: _____
City: _____ State: _____ Zip: _____
Phone number: (_____) _____

Make checks payable to: Special Delivery Publications
To place an order with your Visa, MasterCard
or American Express, call **800-533-8983**
or visit us on line @ **www.whereheartsgather.com**

....

Special Delivery Publications
5109-82nd, Suite 7, #204   Lubbock, TX 79424

Please send _____ copies of When Friends Gather @ $16.95 ea._____
Please send _____ copies of Move Over Martha   @ $10.95 ea. _____
Please send _____ copies of Where Hearts Gather @ $16.95 ea. _____

Postage and Handling per book ----------------------$ 3.00 ea. _____
Subtotal _____
Texas residents add 6.25 % sales tax _____
Total _____
Name:_____ Address: _____
City: _____ State: _____ Zip: _____
Phone number: (_____) _____

Make checks payable to: Special Delivery Publications
To place an order with your Visa, MasterCard
or American Express, call **800-533-8983**
or visit us on line @ **www.whereheartsgather.com**

Please list names and addresses of your favorite stores where you would like to see cookbooks from Special Delivery Publications sold.

_____

_____

_____

_____

_____

_____

_____

_____

_____

···

Please list names and addresses of your favorite stores where you would like to see cookbooks from Special Delivery Publications sold.

_____

_____

_____

_____

_____

_____

_____

_____

_____